This Could Have Been an Email

Delivering professional development to teachers is an exciting opportunity to share strategies and ideas, but how do you ensure your audience will care what you have to say and find it worth their time? In this helpful book, Marcus Stein shows how you can improve your presentations by embracing your personality and relatability, knowing your audience, becoming more flexible, and more.

Throughout the book, he offers actionable strategies for reaching adult learners by catering to their motivations and expertise, using a more flexible model rather than slide deck overkill, refining your delivery style, translating your authentic presentation skills to virtual environments, and revamping your professional growth plan. Each chapter weaves together stories, expert insights, transferable tips, and practical steps for putting what you've learned into action.

Stein's warm tone and engaging anecdotes will leave you feeling ready and inspired to polish your craft. Whether you're an instructional coach leading professional learning for your school, an educator looking to speak at conferences, or a consultant working as a Teacher Trainer, you'll find all the strategies and tips you need to deliver professional development that is meaningful and lasting to teachers.

Marcus Stein focuses on improving educational outcomes through technology integration and professional development. He has 13 years of experience in education, including as a classroom teacher. His current role as the Head of Teacher Success at Kami and his previous position as a Director of Professional Development demonstrate his strategic approach to fostering educational innovation and collaboration.

T0383616

Also Available from Routledge Eye on Education
(www.routledge.com/k-12)

The Freelance Educator: Practical Advice for Starting your Educational Consulting Business
Tinashe Blanchet

Making an Impact Outside of the Classroom: A Complete Guide to the Exciting Job Possibilities for Educators
Starr Sackstein

The Edupreneur's Side Hustle Handbook: 10 Successful Educators Share Their Top Tips
Edited By Lisa Dunnigan, Tosha Wright

Prepared Interviewing for Educators: A Guide for Seeking Employment
Scott Lempka

This Could Have Been an Email

A Teacher Trainer's Guide to Delivering More Meaningful PD

Marcus Stein

Routledge
Taylor & Francis Group

NEW YORK AND LONDON

Designed cover image: Getty images

First published 2025
by Routledge
605 Third Avenue, New York, NY 10158

and by Routledge
4 Park Square, Milton Park, Abingdon, Oxon, OX14 4RN

Routledge is an imprint of the Taylor & Francis Group, an informa business

© 2025 Marcus Stein

Library of Congress Cataloging-in-Publication Data
Names: Stein, Marcus, author.
Title: This could have been an email : a teacher trainer's guide to delivering more meaningful PD / Marcus Stein.
Description: New York, NY : Routledge, 2024. | Includes bibliographical references.
Identifiers: LCCN 2024014335 (print) | LCCN 2024014336 (ebook) | ISBN 9781032518411 (hardback) | ISBN 9781032518251 (paperback) | ISBN 9781003404163 (ebook)
Subjects: LCSH: Teachers--Professional relationships. | Career development. | Adult learning. | Mentoring in education. | Teacher-student relationships.
Classification: LCC LB1775 .S668 2024 (print) | LCC LB1775 (ebook) | DDC 371.102/3--dc23/eng/20240510
LC record available at https://lccn.loc.gov/2024014335
LC ebook record available at https://lccn.loc.gov/2024014336

ISBN: 978-1-032-51841-1 (hbk)
ISBN: 978-1-032-51825-1 (pbk)
ISBN: 978-1-003-40416-3 (ebk)

DOI: 10.4324/9781003404163

Typeset in Palatino
by KnowledgeWorks Global Ltd.

This book is dedicated to every teacher who has sat through professional development that could have been an email.

Contents

Meet the Author

Marcus Stein has had an impressive career focused on improving educational outcomes through technology integration and professional development. He has a background in English Education and a master's degree in Educational Technology Leadership. Stein's journey from being a classroom teacher to becoming a key figure in educational technology highlights his dedication to enhancing teaching and learning. With over  13 years of experience in education, including teaching English Language Arts to various grade levels and leading professional development initiatives, Stein has developed expertise in using technology to enrich education. His current role as the Head of Teacher Success at Kami and his previous position as the Director of Professional Development at AXI Education Solutions demonstrate his strategic approach to fostering educational innovation and collaboration. Stein also co-created, hosted, and produced an original education technology podcast called DAT Podcast, which has helped to amplify the voices of educators around the world. Stein has been actively involved in educational technology conferences worldwide, demonstrating his role as a thought leader in integrating technology with pedagogy to engage and empower educators and students.

Introduction

The purpose of this book is to provide tips and strategies to Teacher Professional Development Facilitators. In an effort to improve the quality of your trainings, this practical guide will suggest enhancing the only factor you directly influence, yourself. Instead of emphasizing on ways to bulldoze widespread issues like lack of time and teacher fatigue, this book is designed to focus on and celebrate you – the person who chooses to lead teacher trainings to an audience of peers who often feel like your "training could have been an email."

It has many names: Professional Development (PD), Professional Learning (PL), Teacher Training, Teacher In-Service, Teacher Institute, Teacher Workshop, and Teacher Upskilling. These are all synonymous terms to describe an essential component of the education industry – the continued education of the classroom teacher.

The facilitator leading these continuing education experiences is the focus of this book. For the sake of consistency, the term Teacher Trainer will be used.

Indeed.com describes a Teacher Trainer as a professional whose "duties include observing and assessing teachers, providing input and advice and creating training workshops" (Indeed.com, 2023). We, "teachers behind the teachers," are required to carry the pedagogical skills to lead both audiences of adult teachers and the children they teach. And the imperativeness of the Teacher Trainer parallels that of the Classroom Teacher. In the United States of America, the Department of Education's Office of Elementary and Secondary Education prioritizes Teacher Trainers by rewarding over $2 billion dollars in grants to states to "improve the quality and effectiveness of teachers, principals, and other school leaders" (Office of Elementary and Secondary Education, 2019). So as long as teachers exist, so will Teacher Trainers.

Yet even with the necessity of the Teacher Trainer, very few teachers are truly satisfied with PD offerings. In 2014, The Bill & Melinda Gates Foundation contracted with the Boston Consulting Group to survey and interview over 1,300 professionals in the education sector. When asked what the ideal PD experience should be like, several themes surfaced. Teachers want to be treated like professionals, and they want their PD to be:

◆ Relevant
◆ Interactive
◆ Sustained Over Time
◆ Delivered by Someone Who Understands Their Experience

Unfortunately, only 29% of the teachers reported being satisfied with PD offerings (Bill & Melinda Gates Foundation, 2014). The good news, though, is that most of the factors that teachers see as ideal can be directly impacted by you, the Teacher Trainer. This book is designed for you to hone in on those factors that teachers want and that you can control.

Why This Book?

First, this book will NOT be a "how-to" on teaching teachers. What this book will be, however, is a resource that will compel you to improve your craft by providing you with real-world narratives, genuine advice, and actionable strategies that you can perform with very little to no red tape involved. The things you'll experience in this book are designed for you to absorb and apply quickly because they all pertain to things you can directly control.

In my 11 years as a Professional Development Facilitator and Consultant, I have trained thousands of teachers around the world mostly with an emphasis on instructional technology best practices. In this time, I have researched, experimented, and reflected on ways to consistently deliver effective PD. In that time, I have learned about the formats, topics, and models that work best for PD. However, after collecting thousands of attendee feedback responses over the years, I noticed that very few of the positive feedback reviews mentioned the training format, the topic, or the model I used in the session. Instead, a resounding majority of teachers responded positively and commented on how much they enjoyed my fun personality and relatable delivery style. I also noticed that the teachers who found me likable were the ones who were more keen to attend follow-up PD sessions. That's when I realized what the field of teacher PD was missing: A resource to help elevate the presenter with practical ideas that embrace personality and relatability. So, that's what this book will share – teacher trainer best practices with less emphasis on the PD itself and more emphasis on you, the presenter.

The Design of the Book

This book is divided into five sections. If you prefer a linear, guided approach to learning, read the book chronologically. However, if one section interests you more than another, you can hop around sections based on your own interests and needs.

The five chapters of this book are listed below, along with their summaries

Chapter 1 – Know Your Audience	Learn how to better adapt your PD delivery by catering more to the motivators of the adult learner.
Chapter 2 – Designing Presentations that Stick	Understand how to shift existing and future PD plans to a more flexible model that caters to the professional expertise of attendees.
Chapter 3 – Mastering Public Speaking	Become a more confident presenter by defining your delivery style and by creating a sustainable rehearsal cadence.
Chapter 4 – Presenting Virtually with Confidence	Translate your authentic presentation skills to asynchronous and synchronous virtual environments.
Chapter 5 – Professional Growth	Revamp your professional growth plan by expanding your ideas of upskilling sources.

Each section will follow the same three-part format with tips interspersed throughout. The section structure is explained below with descriptions of each component.

Personal Narrative: In order to highlight the real-world application of each section's content, the section will begin with an anecdote that shares the implications of applying or not applying a specific presenter quality.

Lessons Learned: This part is the heart of each section. In this portion, the lessons learned from the real-world experience will be explored in depth by providing research from sources like peer-reviewed articles, observations, studies, and live interviews.

Putting it into Action: Each section will end with a series of activities and reflections designed to give you practical actions you can perform using the insights gained from the section. Think of this part like a Teacher Trainer's Improvement Choice Board with a variety of ways to implement the ideas shared.

Transferable Teacher Tips

Each section will also feature Transferable Teacher Tips interspersed throughout. These are bite-sized ideas that work well in the classroom and in the PD space. These signposted moments are typically the easiest concepts to adopt because they mimic the strong teaching that you performed when you were leading students.

Expert Insights

This book also includes interview excerpts from three PD experts who share real-world insights about the most and least successful PD strategies:

◆ Dr. Sara D. Bourgeois
Assistant Professor of Education at Nicholls State University
Director of Center for Teaching Excellence at Nicholls State University

- ◆ Toni Rose Deanon, M.Ed
  Community Engagement, Designated Hype Person at The Modern Classrooms Project
- ◆ Marc Dembowski
  Senior Learning Designer at AVID Center

Enjoy

This book is a combination of my personal experiences and thorough research, carefully crafted to provide you with practical and insightful information. However, my goal is not only to educate you but also to make the journey enjoyable. I want you to have fun while learning and laughing alongside me. Together, we can overcome the dullness that often comes with learning new things by strengthening our skills through engaging and interesting content.

References

Bill & Melinda Gates Foundation. (2014). Teachers Know Best: Teachers' Views on Professional Development. Gates Foundation. Retrieved January 27, 2023, from https://usprogram.gatesfoundation.org/news-and-insights/usp-resource-center/resources/teachers-know-best-teachers-views-on-professional-development

Indeed.com. (2023, September 7). Teacher Trainer Job Description: Top Duties and Qualifications. https://www.indeed.com/hire/job-description/teacher-trainer-job-description

Office of Elementary and Secondary Education. (2019, August 23). Supporting Effective Instruction State Grants—Title II, Part A. https://oese.ed.gov/offices/office-of-formula-grants/school-support-and-accountability/instruction-state-grants-title-ii-part-a/

1

Know Your Audience

By the time I reached my second year as a classroom teacher, I had attended over ten different professional development (PD) workshops. And in that short period of time, I already started to empathize with teachers who would say things like, "I don't even know why they make us come to these PD workshops. This could have been an email."

In the fall 2009 semester, my school sent me to a professional learning workshop titled Capturing Kids' Hearts. With the combination of the session's mushy title and my growing disdain for lackluster PD, the only excitement I experienced was a reprieve from my daily school duties.

The workshop was hosted at a central location in the district with teacher representatives from each school. When I entered the building, I easily found the training room because there was a woman standing near the doorway shaking hands and welcoming each participant. "Well, that's different." I thought to myself. "I've never seen a greeter at a workshop." When I got to the door, the woman outstretched her arm to shake my hand and said "Hi, I'm Sheryl." I shook her hand, said hello back, and entered the large training room with several classroom-like tables. I chose a table in the corner near the wall outlet. I remember feeling bored before the workshop even started. I could not help but be triggered by the previous year's PD sessions that left me feeling uninspired, confused, and frustrated. I was convinced that this would be another day-long lecture that would require an immense amount of coffee and

DOI: 10.4324/9781003404163-1

optimism to make it through. As I got settled, I noticed that Sheryl greeted every person just as she greeted me.

That pessimistic feeling quickly fled me as Sheryl Sheffield, the greeter and veteran teacher turned PD consultant, introduced herself as our workshop facilitator. She explained that greeting us all at the door was intentional; it was her way of opening up to us while also learning our preliminary levels of engagement. I was in awe at her familiar, motherly demeanor. Disarming is the most accurate description of how she set the tone for the day. Instead of immediately diving into the curriculum or drowning us in death by PowerPoint, Sheryl spoke about her teaching journey, her family, and what motivated her to be an educator. She quickly became the everyteacher, a teacher version of the everyman who felt familiar and relatable. It was the first time I had attended a professional learning workshop where the presenter shared her own positionality and motivators. It was also the first time a presenter asked me to reflect on and share my experiences.

After her introduction and tone-setting, our first task was to choose affirmative adjectives that describe us. Sheryl told us we would refer to ourselves and each other in these affirming names by placing the word in front of our first names. The ideas flooded me quickly: Memorable Marcus, Mesmerizing Marcus, Mastery Marcus, etc. And after ruminating for five minutes, it came to me. I would be known as Majestic Marcus. I liked the sound of it, and I liked the idea of sounding and behaving like nobility. Once everyone chose their own descriptive words, Sheryl handed out paper bags and crayons; we were to write our new names largely on the bags and then design the bags however we wished. I spent the following 20 minutes coloring the entire front face of the bag with MAJESTIC MARCUS, and I left the other sides completely blank. Then Sheryl told us the purpose of the bags. She said "These are your affirmation bags. We will staple all of these to a bulletin board, and throughout the day, you are encouraged to write and deposit affirmations to your classmates here today."

My skepticism started to creep back in. I met the other participants that morning, so I thought it would be inauthentic to affirm them because I didn't know much about them. My original sense of pessimism made me completely forget that a few seconds prior, I was highly engaged in the affirming adjectives activity. I was back at square one with my attitude. As index cards and pencils were passed around, I had no clue who I would affirm or when. So, for the next hour leading up to lunch, I somewhat paid attention to Sheryl; every time I saw someone get up and drop an affirmation note into a bag, I thought to myself, "This is dumb. I don't get it. What could they possibly be affirming each other about? We don't even know each other. Besides, I could NEVER do this with my actual students."

When lunchtime came, I walked by my own bag, and I was shocked and intrigued to see notes from other participants! One of the notes stated, "Love your positive spirit, Marcus." And another stated, "You ARE majestic." I bolted to my seat and immediately scribbled a note to two other participants. And it was at that moment that I realized what Sheryl was doing. Undeterred by feelings of apprehension, Sheryl remained positive and open because she was modeling a way to build a positive classroom culture. She motivated and engaged with us by being a relatable, trustworthy peer to us. Because of this, she gathered buy-in quickly. And I had become her biggest fan. I found myself wanting to learn from her.

By the end of the workshop, I fully bought into the Capturing Kid's Hearts curriculum partly because of the quality of the content but mostly because of Sheryl's delivery. An optimistic, authentic, disarming teacher like Sheryl makes it possible to build an audience of engaged learners – both children and adults. By the end of the full three-day workshop with Sheryl Sheffield, I knew I would someday inspire teachers like she did. I knew I wanted to be a presenter like her – someone whose dynamic lesson delivery could never be captured in the confines of an email.

Lesson Learned: Good PD is Much Less about the Content and Much More about the Person Delivering the Content

Think about the most recent PD workshop you attended. Was the upcoming session the top priority for you at the time? How many other things were on your to-do list for that day? How unbiased and focused were you during the session? How quickly did you decide that "this could have been an email instead?" Even if you were the most eager, most focused learner in the room, it's impossible to attend PD completely void of competing adult responsibilities and/or previous impressions of staff trainings. Thus, a key pillar in your journey to elevate your teacher training is accepting three realities that aren't far from those of young learners.

Adults are Highly Distracted, Judge Quickly, and Want to be Treated Like Adults

In an August 2023 *Time Magazine* article, Dr. Margaret Sibley, a professor of psychiatry at the University of Washington School of Medicine, shared that

> Distractibility is nothing new. Focus naturally waxes and wanes depending on a range of factors, from how much sleep someone got the night before to how interested they are in the task at hand. But the "cocktail" of anxieties inherent to modern [adult] life can make for a particularly potent drain on attention.
>
> (Ducharme, 2023)

Modern distractions like cell phones, smartwatches, and unlimited video streaming services will continue to evolve, and so will the ways in which they continue to occupy our attention spans. Couple that reality with the fact that adults carry responsibilities like caring for children and paying bills, and you have a recipe for the prejudice that teachers carry when walking into PD sessions. In the case of the Capturing Kid's Hearts workshop I attended back in 2009, I was highly unfocused and had a growing bitterness for staff in services. I was burned by boring PD workshops in the past, but I was also incredibly anxious about leaving my students in the care of a substitute; it was only my second year teaching, and I knew my below-average classroom management skills would make the substitute's job tough. I wore all of those feelings in the form of sweat on my palms when I shook Sheryl Sheffield's hand. And rather than ignoring the apprehension, she smiled and greeted me genuinely. She also spent time asking about us before the workshop started and shared personal anecdotes about herself. Essentially, she, like many other great presenters, acknowledged the humanism of the teachers before diving into content delivery. And she continued to respect us as humans throughout the workshop by "greeting" us even after the session started.

 Transferable Teacher Tip #1: Plan to Greet

Similar to standing in the hallway of your classroom and greeting students as they enter, position yourself so that you're able to greet teachers with a warm welcome. Reserve time and space in your plans to greet.

Your New Weapon against Pessimistic Preconceptions: The Greeting

Like many captivating presenters, Sheryl Sheffield checked the audience's vibe and built rapport quickly, making it easier to forget our preconceptions and escape distractions. Before teachers enter your professional learning workshop, many have already formed opinions about the session or even you, the presenter. Therefore, it's important for you to make a stellar first impression and build rapport quickly.

In his book *How to Make People Like You in 90 Seconds or Less*, Nicholas Boothman (2008) breaks down the greeting into five parts: Open, Eye, Beam, Hi!, and Lean.

Open. The first part of the greeting is to open your attitude and your body. For this to work successfully, you must have already decided on a positive attitude that's right for you.

Eye. The second part of the greeting involves your eyes. Be first with eye contact. Look this new person directly in the eye. Let your eyes reflect your positive attitude.

Beam. This part is closely related to eye contact. Beam! Be the first to smile. Let your smile reflect your attitude.

Hi! Whether it's "Hi!" or "Hello!" or even "Yo!" say it with a pleasing tonality and attach your own name to it ("Hi! I'm Naomi"). As with the smile and the eye contact, be the first to identify yourself.

Lean. The final part of introducing yourself is the "lean." This action can be an almost imperceptible forward tilt to very subtly indicate your interest and openness (pp. 24–25).

For an extrovert like me, greetings come naturally. I prefer to look others in the eyes when speaking, and I never hesitate to smile or say "heya" first. If you are shy or more introverted, though, greeting others can make you feel anxious or awkward. If you find yourself struggling to be more open or if you avoid looking others in the eyes, remember who you are in the class-room with children. You know how your attitude sets the tone for the students, so remember that the same applies to adult learners. Your salutation can be the optimistic catalyst that quickens attendee buy-in, but only if you prioritize making a positive first impression.

 Transferable Teacher Tip #2: Be the First to Say "Hello!"

Teachers take the lead when greeting students and initiating the lesson, so do the same with adults. Remember that your greeting is both a disarming tool and a way to check the pulse of your learners, so don't wait to be smiled at; smile first.

But There's no Time to Greet

In many instances, we will present a workshop in a space where teachers enter at various times before the start of the session. While some presenters prioritize preparing their instructional materials, the disarming presenter would use this time to greet audience members and build rapport. Your setup time before your session is your greeting time, so get creative with how you greet, and remember that greetings can also be eye contact and/or body language.

- ◆ Walk around and greet people as they get settled in.
- ◆ If refreshments exist, grab some, even if you aren't hungry. This could give you the opportunity to con-tribute to casual conversations or to listen in on partici-pant perspectives outside of the training room setting.

◆ Play some music, but not too loud. Choose songs that won't drown out conversation but would work well in a universal karaoke catalog. Look around the room and folks who sing along or dance. This will help you find common ground without saying a word.

◆ Exude that you love what you do. Scan the room while beaming an authentic, positive smile.

Adults Want to be Treated Like Adults

When rapport is solid, and adult learners are engaged, communication is a breeze. But oftentimes, PD trainers are asked to teach a wide range of teachers with varying levels of rapport and interest. Because of this, it's pivotal to know how to shift from speaking to children to speaking to adults.

Seek a Smooth Transaction of Communication

Have you ever been "shushed" during a training? Have you ever felt patronized by another adult during a training? These are telltale signs of the presenter or surrounding adults relying on communication strategies that may be more effective with children, not adults. Respectfully, I stop talking when shushed, and I disarm when I sense another adult patronizing others, but not without rolling my eyes first. You may have reacted similarly if you've ever been in a situation where a fellow adult has spoken to you like they would a child.

To help you understand the most effective ways to communicate with your adult audience, let's use 20th-century Canadian Psychotherapist Eric Berne's theory of transactional analysis as a framework. Berne proposed that the act of communicating verbally or nonverbally is called a transaction, and transactional analysis is "the method for studying interactions between individuals." According to him, communication happens to and from one of three ego states – Parent, Adult, and Child. Note that these terms do not reference standard, dictionary definitions; instead, Berne defines these states based on our experiences. For instance, the Parent "represents a massive collection of recordings in the brain of external events experienced or perceived." And when we speak as Parents, we're often speaking from a perspective of "we know better because we've been taught this." In contrast, within the Child "are the emotions or feelings which accompanied external events." Essentially, when we speak as Children, we are driven by our feelings related to experiences. Lastly, the "Adult data grows out of the child's ability to see what is different than what he or she observed or felt." This means that Adult communicators maneuver from a more logical, learned perspective – the space you want to live in the most when presenting to adults (Transactional Analysis, 2013).

Be a Complimentary Communicator

If you make a conscious effort to stimulate and respond to conversations from an Adult ego, you are essentially reducing the chance of friction from an emotional Child's response or an "I know better" Adult's response. This Adult-to-Adult conversation is ideal because it helps to avoid a crossed transaction – "when an ego state different than the ego state which received the stimuli is the one that responds." For example, if you were to shush your audience as a Parent would, you might create a crossed transaction where audience members also respond like Parents by saying, "I'm not a child. Don't talk to me like that."

 Transferable Teacher Tip #3: Be a De-escalator

Classroom teachers experience communication conflicts regularly, especially when it comes to student misbehavior. Remember that the best way to calm the conversation is to de-escalate. Maintain a calm communication style when presenting even when conversations become tense.

Unfortunately, stimulating conversation from an Adult ego doesn't guarantee an Adult response. Because teachers arrive at PD with other priorities and emotions, crossed transactions are bound to happen, so be prepared to communicate like an Adult. Table 1.1 shows how unexpected crossed transactions can occur during your sessions.

TABLE 1.1 Crossed communication examples and ideas for how to diffuse them

You	Teacher	What Could be Happening Here?	How Do You Respond?
Says: "Everyone, please login to the platform, and we'll get started with the workshop in 3 minutes."	Thinks: "Who does she think she is? Since when does SHE tell us what to do? She's so annoying."	Prior negative experiences with leaders can sometimes cause teachers to view you as a representation of those past experiences.	Acknowledge where and why a teacher might get this impression, and then pivot back to the task at hand. Maintain your open, beaming attitude throughout.
Emails: "Thanks for attending PD with me. Here are followup resources."	Replies: "Thank you too. In the future, can you share these resources during the PD session? It's something I do when I lead PD, and you should do it too."	When parts of your training feel redundant or irrelevant to attendees, they can sometimes consider your help inferior to their own self-learning journeys.	Decide if responding via email will or won't help you build rapport with the person. If you sense another Parent ego responding to you, fight the urge to respond like a Child and choose a response that compliments the conversation rather than complicates it with a back-and-forth about who knows best.
You: "Anyone have questions or need to see anything again?"	Body language: "I'm just ready to go. I hope we finish early."	For some participants, your workshop can't or won't be a top priority. This causes a buy-in curve that's harder to overcome.	Don't let disengagement or disinterest turn you into a Parent who says things like "This is a mandatory training. We must get through this." Combine your greeting skills with your calm, learned adult perspective and genuinely reinforce the relevancy and value of your PD.

Conversations can get confusing when people are not on the same page. These types of conversations can also lead to misunderstandings. As PD leaders, it is not enough to start conversations and expect everyone to respond like adults. We must also maintain an adult mindset even if others respond with parent or child mindsets. Recognizing these realities is an important step toward improving how we communicate with teachers.

Putting it into Action

Reflect	Explore	Experiment
Create a superhero persona for yourself based on your ideal communicator traits. How can you bring out your inner communication superhero in your interactions with colleagues? What does it take for you to go from Clark Kent to Superman?	Use an AI chatbot like ChatGPT to generate creative ways to improve your andragogy. In your query, use modifiers like "creative" and "out of the box" to generate more innovative ideas.	Create three new ways to get your audience's attention without speaking like a scolding parent or a complaining child ego. Remember that communication can be verbal or nonverbal.

References

Boothman, N. (2008). How to make people like you in 90 seconds or less. Workman Publishing.

Ducharme, J. (2023, August). Why Everyone's Worried About Their Attention Span—And How to Improve Yours. Time. https://time.com/6302294/why-you-cant-focus-anymore-and-what-to-do-about-it/

Transactional Analysis. (2013, January 16). Eric Berne M.D. https://ericberne.com/transactional-analysis/

2

Designing Presentations that Stick

Dizzy was how I remember feeling as I furiously transcribed the content of a live demonstration of Kami, a widely adopted education technology app. In July 2021, I was hired as a full-time Teacher Success Champion there, and my role was to evangelize the app with impactful teacher professional development and support. So, I spent my first days at Kami learning the content of the app's most widely offered teacher trainings: Kami 101. In an effort to clearly define all of the skills included in a basic product training and to create a scalable outline of the content that I and future Teacher Success Champions could replicate, I attempted to transcribe the Kami basics workshop. However, midway through my second observation of the workshop, I could not keep up with documenting my learning and actively participating. My fingers just wouldn't move quickly enough to list all of the skills covered. The presenter was engaging and relatable, and I enjoyed the way he delivered the workshop, but the amount of content was overwhelming. After throwing in the towel on listing all of the skills I was learning, I knew exactly how I would help make Kami's professional development more impactful: I would embark on a mission to shift the company's training and support to a model that focused more on engaging with teachers and less on instructor delivery of content.

DOI: 10.4324/9781003404163-2

At that point in my career, I had spent over six years delivering in-person and virtual professional development sessions in synchronous and asynchronous formats; I worked with hundreds of teachers and teacher leaders to support effective instructional technology integration, and I learned that no teacher arrives at PD completely void of prior knowledge. Sometimes, because of audience expertise, I became a learning facilitator who steered conversations rather than a lecturer who closely dispensed information. I also learned that activating teacher prior knowledge was my ticket to gain audience buy-in. Conjuring audience expertise made the teachers WANT to learn from me, and I found that the more I leaned into activating that knowledge, the easier it was for me to deliver content.

Changing the status quo isn't easy, though. I worked for a company with many brilliant, experienced people who had been delivering training and support years before I joined the team. While I was excited that I quickly diagnosed a way to improve Kami's training offerings, I was also scared. Several scenarios circulated in my head: I thought, "What would happen if I propose the idea of focusing less on content and more on relevance and activating prior learning?" Would I be met with a combative, "Who do you think you are?" What if my idea gets outnumbered by those who prefer emphasizing content completion over teacher buy-in? What if they don't think I have enough evidence to prove my claims? What will I do if someone argues that teaching less content lowers the chance of users maximizing what Kami can do? My brain swirled even further, and I started to think about the many times I had been asked to follow a training script. In previous roles, I was frequently asked to create and adhere to detailed agendas with little room for audience engagement. I remembered what it felt like to be terrified to adjust content or time constraints because I usually co-planned workshops alongside supervisors with more teaching or leadership experience than me. I oftentimes delivered trainings bound by contractual restrictions, so there were instances when I had almost no wiggle room to bond with the teachers.

There was another type of recollection, though, that gave me the audacity to swim upstream and say, "I think we should reconsider the way we deliver Kami 101." An avalanche of positive thoughts flooded me when I spoke up because I recalled the many times I leaned into the audience's prior knowledge and no longer had to be the sole source of information in the room. I remembered the moments when I could breeze through topics because I intentionally embedded time for teachers to be the "professionals" in professional development. My self-assurance grew to the point where I challenged the status quo because I remembered why teachers walked away from trainings saying, "Are YOU gonna be the trainer for the next workshop? I wanna learn from YOU!" Teachers WANT to learn when professional development includes more interaction that emphasizes their experiences; so if we follow this model, there's no need to adhere to strict, instructor-led content outlines.

To my surprise, the suggestion of modifying Kami's training delivery style was met with an open-minded, "We're keen." I had thought so much about the apprehension of making the suggestion that I was almost lost for words when asked, "Can you tell us what you'd do differently and what impacts we might see?" I paused, embraced the open-minded energy of my coworkers, and responded by underscoring what any trainer would want at the conclusion of a workshop: to share meaningful information that sticks. I reiterated that in order to make content stickier, the Teacher Trainer should be allowed to and encouraged to vary the pace and depth of knowledge based on the audience's prior knowledge indicators. I added that interaction and feedback are the strongest, real-time data points that inform when and where to steer the dispelling of information. And after demonstrating what it would look like to deliver interactive training driven by audience insights, Kami decided that I and six new Teacher Success Champions would take over the task of training its users. A year after that first demonstration, the success of the Teacher Success Champions grew to a team of 14 passionate trainers – all former classroom teachers who valued participant insights as the prominent force to drive professional development delivery. With the success of the new training model, we rolled out the updated Kami 101 training to all of our users and the impact was noticeable. Teachers were more engaged in the training, they felt more connected to the app and its potential to improve their teaching, and they were more motivated to implement Kami in their classrooms. The training became an opportunity for teachers to connect with each other and share their experiences, rather than just a lecture on how to use an app. In the end, we all consistently gathered feedback on our fun, relevant, and engaging training styles, and to this day, we are asked to deliver follow-up or repeat sessions to education communities we've worked with previously.

None of this change would have happened, though, if I had not known that activating prior knowledge was the key to making presentations that stick. I knew that content without context was always hard to make sticky. And in the end, that boldness to be outspoken came from studying, experimenting, and observing the positive impacts of professional development driven by the attendees' expertise. It didn't hurt that Kami had an open-minded spirit with a strong desire to improve the lives of teachers.

Lesson Learned: Activating Prior Knowledge and Catering to Adult Learning Styles Reduces the Need for You to Be the Sole Deliverer of Content

Going off-script can be scary. And that's essentially what I'm asking you to do when I suggest allowing the audience to drive content absorption. For some trainers, letting go of being the beholder of information can feel like releasing a guide rope in the desert during a sandstorm. How will you remember the original trail with new conversations flying about? What if you forget where you were in the outline and become unable to get things back on track? The truth is that while you may be the designated leader, you're not the only person who's walked the walk. Therefore, even if you get lost, with clear goals and the ability to conjure audience expertise, plenty of information will be pouring in from your audience that will steer your training to the finish line. To make content more engaging and relevant, we trainers must activate prior knowledge by embracing adult learning theory best practices, by paying attention to real-time feedback cues, and by remixing traditional training outlines.

Letting Go of Being the Only Expert in the Room

When you're incredibly passionate about the content you deliver or plan to share multiple skills or concepts in a workshop, your natural inclination may be to enthusiastically pummel topics at teachers. Sometimes, that enthusiasm transfers to teachers, and you may even walk away successfully addressing every aspect of your training outline. But that doesn't mean that the learnings stick with teachers. In order to align our training plans and behaviors to a mode better received by the adult learner, Teacher Trainers should understand the foundations of good andragogy.

American adult educator Malcolm Knowles popularized the term andragogy in the 1980s to describe the art and science of teaching adults, and facilitators have been using his theories as a guide since. In its "Fact Sheet No. 11: Adult Learning Theories," the Teaching Excellence in Adult Literacy program summarizes Knowles's implications about the adult learner when he says that this age of the student:

♦ Moves from dependency to increasing self-directedness as he/she matures and can direct his/her own learning;

♦ Draws on his/her accumulated reservoir of life experiences to aid learning;

♦ Is ready to learn when he/she assumes new social or life roles;

♦ Is problem-centered and wants to apply new learning immediately; and

♦ Is motivated to learn by internal, rather than external, factors (TEAL Center Staff, 2011).

Simply put, adults are intrinsically motivated students who prefer learning practical skills in a self-directed format. So, that means that if you're planning to closely hold and dispense information by playing the lecturer role, you're already working in opposition to the way in which adults learn best. In order to create effective training plans for adult learners, it's important to accept that you may not always be the expert in the room. By adopting this mindset, you'll be able to tailor your plans to their unique needs and preferences, resulting in a more engaging and successful learning experience.

Three Reasons Why You Should Be Spending Less Time Building Slide Decks

Artificial Intelligence

Before the launch of artificial intelligence chatbots like ChatGPT, a large part of presentation curation and design relied on carefully crafted outlines and manually constructed deliverables. Now that we have an AI model "trained on a staggering 175 billion parameters," we're able to draw inspiration from and draft example training materials with a series of trainer-created prompts. In his 2023 *Forbes* article "A Short History of ChatGPT: How We Got to Where We Are Today," contributor Bernard Marr shares how AI chatbots like ChatGPT have already disrupted our usual processes. Marr declares that ChatGPT-3's "advanced text-generation capabilities led to widespread use in various applications, from drafting emails and writing articles to creating poetry and even generating programming code. It also demonstrated an ability to answer factual questions and translate between languages" (Marr, 2023). This means that with the right prompting, Teacher Trainers now have a place to remix and rethink existing training resources into formats that fit the relevancy and needs of new teacher audiences.

Plentiful Existing Resources Online

In addition to the influence of AI, the COVID-19 global pandemic has shifted the way we plan for PD. Because there has been a rapid shift toward classroom technology integration and virtual professional development, teachers and trainers have been able to access learning resources anytime, anywhere. This has made it easier to locate and remix exemplars, templates, outlines, and other resources. In fact, several sites offer free, readymade templates. Slidescarnival.com and Slidesmania.com are websites that host various presentation templates in PowerPoint, Google Slides, and Canva editable file formats. Canva.com not only provides templates but also offers Magic Design, which uses AI to design slides and content based on provided prompts.

Slide Decks are Low-Yield Aspects of Planning PD

In the 1970s, The ADDIE Instructional Design Model was developed at Florida State University. ADDIE is an acronym for Analysis, Design, Development, Implementation, and Evaluation. Each phase is intended to produce information, plans, or products that affect the character, content, and instruction experience, one step at a time. In this model, emphasis is placed on the Analysis and Design components as the most essential parts of preparing presentations because audience research is what creates the most relevant, aligned creation of workshop deliverables. And when trainings are completed, the ADDIE Model highly encourages Teacher Trainers to evaluate effectiveness to better align future sessions. With that being said, only ⅕ of the ADDIE Model (Development) compels presenters to reflect on the materials they plan to use during trainings. Thus, if a trainer is prioritizing the full breadth of their training preparation time into the steps of the ADDIE Model, the creation of slides is realistically a minor, low-yield aspect of the workshop planning process (Ritzhaupt & Covello, 2017).

Given the rapid development of AI, the growth of free resource repositories, and the higher-impact pillars of the ADDIE model, this chapter will provide fewer tips on curating and creating presentation materials. To help you design presentations that stick, we'll focus more on planning and preparation strategies that can't be solved by AI or with an existing, readymade template; this chapter will help you design and remix training plans by emphasizing observations only you can note and real-time adjustments only you can make.

Transferable Teacher Tip #4: Don't Reinvent the Wheel

Classroom teachers are expert hunters and gatherers when it comes to sourcing readymade instructional materials. The same applies to teacher leaders. The next time you're charged with delivering an original training session, search the internet first. There's a high likelihood that you'll at least find a starting point of inspiration.

Research Precedes Design

The more you can surmise about the teachers you will instruct, the easier it is to determine the relevance and potential stickiness of your presentation. The ebook *ADDIE Explained* shares four easy-to-understand outcomes of planning your sessions. At the end of your analysis, you should be able to produce the following:

1. Needs Analysis: A description of the problem and learning goal(s) to be achieved.
2. Learner Analysis: A description of the learners in terms relevant to instruction.
3. Context Analysis: A description of the conditions and timeframe under which the learned skills, knowledge, or attitude would be applicable.
4. Task Analysis: An explication of a task, performance, or demonstration according to sequences, priorities, decisions, choices, and alternatives.

In order to gather and collate participant information quickly, this data can be collected with and without prompting. For example, you may already know the audience subject and grade level expertise for a group of teachers you will be leading, and therefore, there is no need to prompt them about their demographics. Additionally, when we have a specific timeframe to work with, we begin building a Context Analysis to ensure our content fits within the given time constraint. However, to conduct thorough research on teachers, pre-training surveys with intentional prompts are necessary to construct your Needs Analysis, Learner Analysis, Context Analysis, and Task Analysis.

TABLE 2.1 Pre-training survey sample questions

Prompt	This Data Helps Inform…
Name + Email	Learner Analysis: How to get in touch with teachers outside of the training
Current Teaching Grade Level(s) and Subject Area(s)	Learner Analysis: What types of examples parallel the audience's grade levels and subject areas
Something You Already Know About (Insert Topic)	Context Analysis: Teacher prior knowledge levels
Something You Want to Know About (Insert Topic)	Task Analysis: Teacher interests
What are some of the biggest roadblocks or hurdles to your or your students' success?	Needs Analysis: Relevant problems that could potentially be solved with your training

The best way to send and collect these data is by using a free digital form service such as Google Forms, Microsoft Forms, or Survey Monkey (Table 2.1).

If you aren't aware of who your participants will be or if there isn't enough time or data to research your audience, then you can perform a pulse check at the start of your presentation. If this is the route you take, remember to carve out time in your session prompt and gather this information from your audience. Without knowing basic background information, you run a higher risk of your presentation being irrelevant.

Rethinking Presentation Design through the Lens of a Teacher Education Professor: Dr. Sara D. Bourgeois

One weekend in the spring of 2023, after chatting about our plans for the next episode of our co-created podcast, Assistant Professor of Education at Nicholls State University Dr. Sara D. Bourgeois and I branched into a discussion about the noticeable changes she observes most about her class of teacher candidates. In that brief, tangential conversation, I learned more about the potential behaviors of future teachers and the shifting priorities of a college professor aiming to better engage with a modern audience of adult learners.

Dr. Sara D. Bourgeois's approach to teaching adult learners emphasizes the role of authenticity in the educational process. She believes that by sharing personal experiences, especially challenges, educators can forge deeper connections with their students. This method stands in contrast to the often detached and impersonal atmosphere found in higher education settings, where students are sometimes viewed merely as recipients of information rather than as whole individuals with complex lives outside of the classroom. Bourgeois argues that recognizing the personal lives and experiences of adult learners can significantly enrich the learning environment, making it more inclusive and supportive.

When asked how this approach and years of teaching have changed the way she prepares and presents to her adult students, Dr. Sara D. Bourgeois commented on how much more engaging lessons have been since de-prioritizing content creation and lesson scripting:

> I have noticed that there is more interaction during teaching or presenting than there was when I first started teaching. Initially, I used to stick to a script and did not encourage much interaction from the audience. However, now I feel that there are more opportunities for the audience to interact and participate. I ask questions and students respond, leading to engaging discussions. Even when presenting to teachers, there is a lot more interaction and conversation that takes place. I no longer rely on a script and slides, but instead, I encourage interaction and go with the flow of the discussion.

Bourgeois's teaching philosophy includes a strong stance against the imposter syndrome that many educators and students alike may experience. She advocates for an environment where vulnerability is seen as a strength, allowing both teachers and students to grow together through shared experiences. This approach not only helps in building a stronger teacher-student relationship but also promotes a learning atmosphere that is engaging, interactive, and deeply impactful. By embodying authenticity and allowing personal stories to inform teaching practices, educators can create a more dynamic and effective educational experience for adult learners.

Transferable Teacher Tip #5: Let the Conversation Meander ... Just a Little

It happens all the time in the classroom – an excited student's discussion veers off into a tangent. This happens with adult learners too. Instead of immediately stifling the excitement, allow the moment of joy to fill the room before getting the conversation back on track.

Your Audience is Signaling When to Adjust Pace and Depth, but Are You Prepared to Shift?

How can you know if your professional development workshops are consistently effective and engaging? Ask your audience! Because your audience members are teachers, they will have no problem identifying the parts of your instructions that are and aren't working. But to get that information from your audience, you have to prompt them with the right questions and pay attention to nonverbal cues.

Ad Hoc Check-ins

Prompted feedback can be done in the form of paper forms, digital surveys, or informal Q&A. Going paperless with digital feedback forms tends to be the most impactful because they can sort your feedback and provide faster insights into your strengths and weaknesses as a presenter. Even though many presenters employ digital feedback forms, we often use those as post-training tools because we don't want to give up live teaching time for teachers to load an online form, respond to our questions, and wait while we interpret and action their responses. This process of midpoint surveying doesn't have to be time-consuming or disruptive to the flow of learning, especially if the presenter uses relevant prompts with binary

TABLE 2.2 Example audience prompts for ad hoc check-ins

Audience Prompt	Informs a Shift In...
On a scale of 1–5, how confident would you feel if you had to replicate the skill I just taught?	Depth of content
Yes or No: I have some experience with this topic or strategies	Audience-led instruction
Yes or No: I have learned at least one helpful thing I can use in my classroom so far	Depth of content
Yes or No: I am able to hear and understand the presenter	Pace of delivery

or Likert-scale responses. Easy-to-visualize prompts simplify the process of collecting data that inform the pace, depth, and leader of your next instructional activity; so, as you become more intentional at using live audience responses to drive your training outline, remember to keep prompts brief (Table 2.2).

Nonverbal Noticings

Checking in with teachers throughout your sessions can be an effective way to save your PD from becoming one of those that could have been an email, but it doesn't always require prompting. As you move from activity to activity in your trainings, teachers are constantly responding nonverbally. It's up to you, though, to remember to look for and respond to these nonverbal noticings. This means you cannot stand and deliver PD without observing and responding to your audience. This means that you'll have to pay attention to how teachers behave in response to your instruction (Table 2.3).

 Transferable Teacher Tip #6: If Possible, Study Your Roster

Each year, classroom teachers receive rosters of students and some form of their previous education information. The same applies to the rosters of teachers who sign up for your training sessions. If you can capture audience information before the training, research their subject areas, grade levels, extracurricular involvement, and accolades. These are all potential relevancy drivers for your scheduled training.

TABLE 2.3 Nonverbal teacher cues and possible interpretations

Nonverbal Cue	Possible Interpretation
Smiling or laughing	You're making a connection. Your audience is conformable with you being the leader of information.
Leaning Forward	You're spot on. Your audience is finding intrigue and relevancy with your pace, depth, and leadership and are more keen for you to increase complexity.
Not looking at you or your presentation	Your content is either too simple or too complex, and your audience is missing how it personally connects to them.
Frustrated or Confused	The pace of your instruction is either too slow or too fast. Your audience cannot see themselves replicating what you're doing.
On-topic side conversations	If the audience is discussing the topic, this is an indicator that they should be the content delivery leader.
Off-topic side conversations	If the audience is not discussing the topic, this is an indicator that both your content depth and pace should be adjusted.

The Simpler the Outline, the Easier it is to Reconfigure to Meet Real-Time Needs

Your training outline format can be listed as detailed as you wish, but at minimum, it should take into consideration the research from your Analysis and the parameters defined in your Design phases of the ADDIE Model Instructional Design Process. These two components dictate the contents of the third phase of the ADDIE Model, Development. This is the part of professional development construction that trainers are most familiar with – especially when it comes to remixing readymade iterations of workshops.

Regardless of the training outline origin, the agenda is always linear – a Teacher Trainer seeking to take a group of teachers from low to high performance on a specific skill or strategy. And this is no different in classrooms as teachers embark on journeys to success every day. But as we have learned, adult learners like to take the lead, and they learn best when their expertise is valued. That means that if a Teacher Trainer wants to plan for more engaging PD sessions, the pathway should not be linear. Teacher experiences and your relevance to them are unearthed during your presentations and can branch your instruction in

TABLE 2.4 Template for a 30-minute living training agenda

Minutes	Content	Leader	Depth	Pace
5	Introduction + Housekeeping	**Trainer**/ Audience	Surface/**Mid**/ In-depth	Quick/**Moderate**/ Slow
10	Direct Instruction	Trainer/ Audience	Surface/Mid/ In-depth	Quick/Moderate/ Slow
5	Guided Practice	Trainer/ Audience	Surface/Mid/ In-depth	Quick/Moderate/ Slow
5	Independent Practice	Trainer/ Audience	Surface/Mid/ In-depth	Quick/Moderate/ Slow

an infinite amount of directions. This creates learning journeys that resemble winding Etch-A-Sketch drawings. To plan for changes in your presentation depth, pace, and leader, use a living outline that has room for you to designate adjustments in your plans based on real-time audience discoveries. A living training outline only makes assumptions in the first couple of minutes of the presentation because the Teacher Trainer typically leads with some form of introduction. Beyond that, the remaining contents of the agenda shift based upon the audience insights gained during the training. Simply stated, the living agenda reminds you to periodically adjust the content leader, depth, and pace throughout your trainings. (Table 2.4).

Putting it into Action

Reflect	Explore	Experiment
Perform a rigidity check on your most recent training. As you presented, how frequently did you adjust your pace or depth of content delivery? How often did the audience lead instruction? What adjustments can you make in the future to plan for a less linear delivery of information?	Use an AI chatbot to search for more easy-to-visualize audience prompts that you can use during trainings. Which prompts tend to yield the most informative insights while being the least disruptive to the flow of your workshop?	Choose a nonverbal audience cue to look for in your next training. Try responding to the cue in more than one way. Which response was the most effective? Why do you think so?

References

Marr, B. (2023, May 19). A Short History of ChatGPT: How We Got to Where We Are Today. Forbes. https://www.forbes.com/sites/bernardmarr/2023/05/19/a-short-history-of-chatgpt-how-we-got-to-where-we-are-today/?sh=20bdeca674f1

Ritzhaupt, A. D., & Covello, S. (2017). ADDIE explained. University of New Hampshire. https://pressbooks.usnh.edu/addieexplained/

TEAL Center Staff. (2011). TEAL center fact sheet no. 11: Adult learning theories. LINCS | Adult Education and Literacy | U.S. Department of Education. https://lincs.ed.gov/state-resources/federal-initiatives/teal/guide/adultlearning

3

Mastering Public Speaking

During the fall 2014 semester, I experienced the worst, most jarring moment in my professional learning career. While the experience was alarming, though, it DID significantly strengthen my speaking skills. That year, I worked as a part-time high school English teacher and a part-time instructional technology coach for a small school district of seven schools. To date, this was the most fulfilling role I've played in my career because I could satisfy my passion for teaching children and adults in the same workday.

My confidence multiplied because I could speak to teachers from a place of practical implementation. Every tip, trick, or tool I shared would be something that I had vetted with my students. And because I walked the walk alongside the teachers in the district, I grew sure of what I said when I spoke to them. I held a high level of relatability with the teachers because I was teaching the same demographic of students as them with the same tools that they had in their classrooms. Therefore, when I was offered an opportunity to lead a mini workshop at an after-school staff meeting, I knew exactly what I wanted to share and why. Recently, I received high marks on my formal classroom observation because I used the students' real-time, online responses to guide my instruction. I wanted all staff members to know my secret to a high observation score because every teacher and student was outfitted with the same equipment and potential as me and my students, I decided to lead a session about checking

DOI: 10.4324/9781003404163-3

for understanding using online polling tools that make student responses visible. Additionally, the faculty did not know this then, but a month before the staff meeting, I flew to Los Angeles, CA, to be a contestant on the game show *Wheel of Fortune*. So, when I coupled that on-camera confidence with the fact that I was presenting in front of teachers who I taught alongside, the perfect self-assurance combination was created. These were my people. And I LOVE the spotlight. Nothing could shake me… or so I thought.

When the staff training day came, about 60 faculty members filled the large group tables in the campus library. I stood in the front of the room next to the principal, and I beamed as the administration shared their housekeeping updates at the start of the meeting. The Wi-Fi was consistent all day, most of the staff arrived with their MacBooks, and the giant screen in the front of the room worked seamlessly. So, when the microphone was passed to me, I dove in immediately.

"Hey friends," I started. "I want to try something new with you all that I think you'll find easy and useful in your classrooms. It got me really positive feedback on my most recent classroom observation." I then changed the screen to display my presentation which was a single page with a prompt and instructions on how to respond. After being displayed for a few seconds, teachers started responding to my prompt: "Share one good thing happening in your life." I was delighted and impressed with how quickly teachers followed instructions and how honest their responses were. On the large screen I was using to lead the session, the staff observed each others' responses with smiles and nods. I was excited to see that many of my team members were simply happy to wake up and inspire children another day. Others commented on their upcoming vacations, birthdays, and anniversaries. And as the responses populated the screen, I read some of them aloud and asked teachers to expand on what made these things good. And just before I was able to make the turn and express how this type of practice would work well to check for student understanding, it happened. Displayed largely in the center of the screen were the letters "IDC." I was shocked by the blatant message of disrespectful disinterest. Under my breath,

I uncontrollably whispered, "What grown adult would do that during a PD?"

I was stunned that someone on the same staff as me in an audience where I thought I had the most credibility would declare "I don't care" during an all-staff training. I attended my fair share of lackluster PD sessions delivered by meek presenters, so I have rolled my eyes and thought to myself, "I don't care" throughout the course of a PD session. But I never thought a person (much less my own co-worker) would express that they didn't care during the training with me. Every bit of confidence I had at the start of the session left me. My natural smile quickly became a forced smirk as my brain computed what to say or do. I was flustered with feelings of embarrassment, anger, and confusion. The person who submitted that response wanted me to know that my workshop was meaningless, and that's precisely what I felt – like what I was saying and how I was saying it meant nothing. How was I going to get my mind back on track? What was I going to do if the audience erupts after noticing the "IDC" on the screen?

When I came to after a minute or so of staring at the "IDC," on the screen, I realized the staff was still responding. The majority of the room was engaged in the content of my session even though I was experiencing a moment of speechlessness. Most of the teachers in the room were still primed to receive my lesson on quickly gathering student feedback. However, as my speaking confidence dwindled, my confidence as a classroom teacher rose to the surface. The classroom teacher in me knew that some learners are less motivated and can even sometimes be downright defiant. But just because a single student or sect of students are not keen to learn doesn't mean the teacher should slow, halt, or lower the quality of instruction for the other students. A good teacher who's "with it" could issue a quick, almost unnoticeable desist and keep the room centered on learning. So that's what I did.

I acknowledged the "IDC" by announcing, "This happens, y'all. We have a learner who didn't follow instructions. This learner also wrote something that could be seen as disrespectful." And then I turned off the anonymous view of the student responses to reveal that it was one of the school's athletic coaches who posted the term. Before he could change his response, I stated,

> Coach here was just modeling what would happen if a student did this. Thanks, Coach. If a student posts something off-task or inappropriate, don't panic. Because the results are visible, we can snapshot this moment and hold the student accountable at our next conference – it's that simple y'all.

I moved on to lead (most of) the audience by underscoring all of the usage cases teachers could apply to the concept of real-time student polling. And (most of) the audience left with positive takeaways. There were also a few staff members who applauded my handling of the often ornery athletic coach.

The truth is that I remained bitter about the "IDC" interjection days after it happened. I took it personal, and I felt attacked. But, I did not let those negative feelings prevent me from celebrating the steadfastness of my presentation. I overcame an unexpected, real-time hurdle, and my ability to communicate my message minimally faltered. It was this moment in my professional development leadership career that made me realize that a large part of my public speaking strength comes from my strong communication skills in the classroom.

Lesson Learned: By Recalling Your Exceptional Teaching Skills, You can Build Unshakeable Public Speaking Skills

I still get jittery before teaching a group of teachers, especially when it's my first time meeting them. Sometimes, I even question whether or not I'm worthy of leading the group I'm about to present to. This doubt that many of us experience is largely called imposter syndrome. *Merriam-Webster's Dictionary* defines imposter syndrome as "a psychological condition that is characterized by persistent doubt concerning one's abilities or accomplishments accompanied by the fear of being exposed as a fraud despite evidence of one's ongoing success" (Definition of Imposter Syndrome, n.d.). And this doubt coupled with existing public speaking fears can make it tough to stay cool and calm as a presenter. However, by drawing confidence from previous experiences, rehearsing frequently, and striving for authenticity, anyone can become a competent and confident public speaker.

You're Already a Public Speaker

If you've ever taught a group of students, you're already a public speaker. You know what it means to be a compelling communicator. You know what to do when things don't go as planned like when a fire alarm completely disrupts your lesson or when you have to teach in the dark because a storm knocked out the power in your classroom. So, why is it that many of us are terrified to speak in front of groups of adults?

Lack of Experience

Think back to your first year as a classroom teacher. How anxious were you then? How long did it take you to start lessons without the new teacher jitters? Leading PD can be a similar feeling. At first, the experience can feel intimidating delivering training to a group of your peers, many of whom are older and have more experience in the classroom than you. However, just like your nerves calmed with every lesson you taught, so will your apprehension about being a master at public speaking.

Your Inner Saboteur

Imposter syndrome, along with other doubtful and pessimistic thoughts about speaking in front of adults, originates from the same place – your inner saboteur, the overly doubtful person in your head trying to convince you that you'll fail. Overcoming these thoughts can be challenging, especially if you've had negative experiences leading trainings in the past. However, it's important to remember that these feelings are not new. You've experienced waves of doubt from your inner saboteur throughout your lifetime, and those waves will continue to crash into you. In order to prevent drowning in those waves, though, speak more confidently by remembering that you interact with adults regularly; you know how to converse with them just like you do with parents when discussing student performance.

The Shift in Situation

Now that you're a Teacher Trainer, not only will you be asked to deliver trainings to classroom teachers, but also other coaches, departmental chairs, supervisors, and even district-level leaders. These situations can apply a heavy sense of pressure as many of these leaders have priorities and experiences that differ from yours. You also may find yourself presenting in unfamiliar spaces with logistical hurdles like poor acoustics or lack of internet. When you feel the weight of unfamiliarity, recall your teaching days and what gave you confidence even during formal observations – your skills. You have the ability to perform even when you fear the pressure of presenting in new spaces with new faces in the room; so, don't let the shifting of your training situations make you forget the successful days in your constantly evolving classroom.

So if we know these hurdles to public speaking mastery are commonplace, how do we overcome them? **The first step is to accept that the fears are real.** In the textbook *Messages that Matter: Public Speaking in the Information Age – Third Edition*, authors Josh Misner and Geoff Carr explain this essential first step in building your confidence as a speaker:

> All too often, novice speakers make the mistake of thinking they need to conquer or overcome their fear, but that type of thinking can set a speaker up for failure. Fear is a necessary component of public speaking. Fear is part of what makes a human human. It can keep people alert and provide them with necessary energy. Above all, it makes the speaker care about how well he or she perform. In public speaking an old saying goes: "Speakers who say they are as cool as a cucumber usually give speeches about as interesting as a cucumber." Overconfidence has probably flattened more potentially interesting and engaging speeches than nervousness ever has.
>
> (Misner & Carr, 2023)

Transferable Teacher Tip #7: Teacher Mode: Activate!

You're not shy when it comes to leading a group of young people, so try to use that same confidence when speaking in front of adults. The core of your confidence in public speaking is the same as the one that helped you excel in teaching students in the classroom.

Practice May Never Make You Perfect, but It'll Always Make You More Confident

As silly as it feels, rehearsing by presenting in the mirror, watching self-recorded videos of your presentations, and testing your pacing and depth with friends are all effective ways to become a master of public speaking; this is mainly because "speakers who practice until they have the confidence to know what to say in a number of different ways eliminate the uncertainty of forgetfulness and the anxiety of humiliation by saying the wrong thing or not knowing what to do" (Misner & Carr, 2023). Simply stated, the more you rehearse (especially in the space where you will be instructing), the more confident you become.

Like an athlete preparing for a competition, though, we often need to focus on specific muscles or skills to get our entire bodies in the best shape to win. So, instead of trying to rehearse every part of every presentation, try using a practice schedule that rotates what you focus on each time you rehearse; as you feel confident with each focus, combine them to deliver a full dress rehearsal. If you're short on time or unable to do multiple practice rounds, try practicing in front of three peers and ask each peer to focus on a different topic during your rehearsal. After your rehearsal, you can work with each peer to discuss a different rehearsal focus and get feedback to improve your presentation skills (Table 3.1).

Keep it Real

When I was 18 years old and a Freshman in college, one of the first clubs or organizations I joined was the competitive speech and debate team. I already had two years of experience competing in interpretive reading and acting on the high school

TABLE 3.1 Training rehearsal schedule with specified delivery focus topics

	Rehearsal Focus	Rehearsal Method	Rehearsal Checklist
Round 1	Timing, Pace, Content	Watch a recording of you leading a training.	◆ Are you satisfied with the amount of content you're able to deliver under the specified time constraints? ◆ Do you have concerns about moving too quickly or too slowly? ◆ Does the content need to be adjusted to make room for activities or pacing changes?
Round 2	Relevance and Interaction	Deliver your training to a peer.	◆ How much of your content applies to the needs of your audience and how easily can they apply your teachings? ◆ Is a majority of your training interaction with the audience or direct instruction? ◆ Does your content need to be made more relevant?
Round 3	Authenticity	Present your training to a sample audience.	◆ When you teach, do you feel like you? Sound like you? Act like you? ◆ Have you embedded personal connections and passion into the session? ◆ Does the content need to be made more authentic to the way you teach?

circuit, and I felt confident that I could translate those skills to the even more competitive, university environment. One of the first activities our coach had the team perform was for us all to take the "Animal in You" test. He shared that this personality test would help us understand and nurture our personality archetypes while also learning how to thrive and coexist with the other animals in the jungle. After a few minutes and very little hesitation in my responses, the test concluded that I was a lion. The more I read the description and rationale, the more I realized what type of speaker I was: "Moving with the unruffled calm of a cat and the dignified gait of someone in command, lions have no need to walk or talk quickly since they're never in danger of being ignored or marginalized" (Otto & Thornton, n.d.). It was as if I had looked up the definition of outgoing and my name was listed as a synonym. I discovered a term to embody my way of speaking, and it immediately made me feel affirmed. Embracing the lion archetype also helped me to receive and adapt to criticism from others. When my coaches would tell me to slow down or speak more quietly, instead of taking offense to the feedback, I was agreeable to the feedback and eager to explore new ideas because I often roar like a lion when my message would be more effectively received if spoken like a calm, eloquent dove.

Defining your self-image and adhering to your authentic version requires a large amount of introspection. In her January 2024 Toastmasters.org blog titled "Cultivating Authenticity as a Speaker," Elizabeth Danziger underscores the amount of effort required to be authentic when she states that "developing self-knowledge begins with having the courage to see yourself as you really are, including your imperfections, doubts, and fears" (Danziger, 2024). This means that as you start to dive deeper and deeper into the layers that comprise your persona, you will be inundated with affirmations while simultaneously being confronted with your traits that hinder the confident delivery of your content.

If you are struggling to find your authentic self, taking personality tests can be a great starting point. These tests can help you understand your strengths, weaknesses, and preferences, which can build your self-awareness and enable you to communicate more effectively with others. By knowing your personality type, you can tailor your communication style to better connect with your audience, and thus increase the chances of your message being understood and retained (Table 3.2).

As you continuously grow confident in the way you define your personality and instructional delivery style, it's important not to misuse your authenticity as a ticket to justify saying and doing whatever you wish during your trainings. In fact, true

authenticity includes emotional intelligence, which dictates that we should only share our thoughts when our audience

TABLE 3.2 List of free personality surveys and inventories

Personality Test Name and URL	Description
Animal in You Animalinyou.com	This assessment uses animal analogies to describe personality traits. Participants are categorized into different animals, like a bear, lion, or dolphin, based on their responses, reflecting various aspects of human personality. Using animal metaphors makes it an engaging and relatable way to explore personality traits.
16 Personalities 16personalities.com	Based on the Myers-Briggs Type Indicator (MBTI), this assessment categorizes individuals into one of the 16 personality types. Each type combines four dichotomies (Introversion/Extraversion, Sensing/Intuition, Thinking/Feeling, and Judging/Perceiving). It's unique for its depth and detailed descriptions of each personality type, including strengths, weaknesses, career paths, and relationship dynamics.
The Predictive Index go1.predictiveindex.com/	Often used in professional settings, the Predictive Index focuses on workplace behaviors and motivations. It helps understand how an individual will likely deal with job-related situations, teamwork, and management styles. This tool is particularly unique for its application in human resources and team dynamics within a professional context.
The Hogwarts Sorting Ceremony wizardingworld.com/sorting-hat	This assessment, inspired by J.K. Rowling's *Harry Potter* series, sorts individuals into one of the four Hogwarts houses (Gryffindor, Hufflepuff, Ravenclaw, and Slytherin). Each house represents a set of personality traits and values, making it unique for its connection to the popular literary world and how it links personality types to the fictional characteristics of each Hogwarts house.
Enneagram Personality Test enneagramuniverse.com/enneagram/test/	The Enneagram is a model of human psychology that describes nine fundamental personality types. Each type is interconnected and can change over time or under stress. This assessment is unique for its focus on emotional and mental health, personal development, and the dynamic nature of personality traits. It is often used for self-discovery and personal growth.

is able to hear and understand them. For example, if you strongly disagree with something another speaker says, you can respectfully state your alternative view without sharing a negative opinion of the other person.

(Danziger, 2024)

Remembering that your authenticity requires frequent checks for relevancy and appropriation will help you maintain audience-appropriate iterations of your authentic self where each version is a form of you that is relevant and appropriate for unique audience groupings.

 Transferable Teacher Tip #8: Lost? Find Your Anchor

In the classroom, anchor charts are visual resources that help keep the learning on track. Use this same strategy when you're speaking to teachers. If you fear getting lost in your training, create an easy-to-access visual to remind you of your main points.

A Word from the Realest Person I Know: Toni Rose Deanon

I chatted with Toni Rose Deanon, Community Engagement for the Modern Classrooms Project in the fall of 2023. In the interview, they underscored the crucial role of authenticity in effective public speaking, particularly when engaging adult learners. Their insights revealed that being authentic is not just a communicative strategy, but a fundamental aspect of connecting with and effectively educating adults.

Deanon exemplified authenticity through their willingness to be vulnerable and transparent with their audience. This was evident when they shared an anecdote about starting a webinar by openly admitting, "Hey yeah I just woke up a minute ago. So I'm a little bit messy right now, but we gon get through it together." Such candidness broke the conventional barriers between the speaker and the audience, fostering a sense of relatability and trust. By embracing their imperfections and being genuine, Deanon created an environment of authenticity and openness that made their audience feel comfortable and engaged. Their approach is an excellent reminder that being honest and transparent can help build stronger connections with others.

Further emphasizing the importance of authenticity, Deanon discussed how they managed their interactions by prioritizing the emotional state of her audience. They noted the significance of acknowledging how participants felt at the beginning of a session: "We're gonna start off with how are you feeling? And we're gonna name it. And it's okay however you show up." This approach not only demonstrated empathy but also reinforced the idea that authentic communication involves the understanding and addressing of the real-time emotional context of the audience.

Additionally, Deanon's approach to feedback and reflection showcased their authentic engagement with public speaking. They expressed a readiness to admit mistakes and learn from them: "I'm also really quick at reflecting and catching myself, and I welcome feedback. Hey did I say some messed up thing? That's okay. I'm gonna apologize, acknowledge, and then do better next time." This openness to learning and improvement was a part of their leaning into authenticity, as it showed a genuine commitment to personal and professional growth.

In essence, Toni Rose Deanon's perspective highlighted authenticity as a key driver of effective public speaking. Their strategies – being open about their own experiences, prioritizing the emotional well-being of their audience, and embracing a reflective and responsive approach to feedback – all served to illustrate how authenticity can powerfully resonate with and engage adult learners (Deanon, personal communication, November 13, 2023).

 Transferable Teacher Tip #9: QTIP (Quit Taking it Personally)

From the way we dress to the way we pronounce certain words, our students find ways to disrupt or even poke fun at us, but we never take it personally. "They're kids," we often say to ourselves. Apply this same level of grace when your trainings get disrupted. Don't take it personally. Stay confident, and deliver that lesson!

Putting it into Action

Reflect	Explore	Experiment
Become a fear fighter by first listing your top three public speaking fears. Next, list the top three things teachers value about your training. The next time one of your fears creeps in, fight them by reminding yourself of your top three points of value.	Search YouTube for other Teacher Trainers confidently discussing similar topics as you. How can you tell the person is confident? Which strategies from Chapter 3 do you think the presenter has used to become a confident speaker?	Instead of rehearsing your presentations in first person, try practicing them as narratives told in the third person point of view. As the narrator of your presentation, diagram your story's plot by clearly defining the conflict, rising action, climax, falling action, and conclusion. What new thoughts surface when you think of your presentation in plot sequence format?

References

Danziger, E. (2024, January). Cultivating Authenticity as a Speaker. Toastmasters.org. https://www.toastmasters.org/magazine/magazine-issues/2024/jan/cultivating-authenticity

Deanon, T. R. (2023, November 13). [Interview by M. Stein].

Definition of Imposter Syndrome. (n.d.). Merriam-webster.com. Retrieved January 29, 2023, from https://www.merriam-webster.com/dictionary/impostor%20syndrome

Misner, J., & Carr, G. (2023). Messages that matter: Public speaking in the information age – third edition. North Idaho College. https://nic.pressbooks.pub/messagesthatmatter/

Otto, M., & Thornton, J. (n.d.). Animal in You. Animalinyou.com. Retrieved February 7, 2023, from https://www.animalinyou.com/animals/lion/

4

Presenting Virtually
with Confidence

The initial joy of working from home alongside my two dogs faded about a month into the COVID-19 global pandemic; I started to feel like it was becoming harder and harder to genuinely smile and love training teachers because I missed the in-person interactions I grew to thrive on. As an extrovert, the pandemic was excruciatingly painful to endure without the thing that gives me the most life – other people.

Since I was a child, I've been known for my extroverted personality. My mom often shares a story from when I was four years old that highlights this trait. She recalls being asked to stay back when picking me up from daycare one day. Mrs. Robinson, the daycare owner, with a smile, revealed to my mother that I was the daycare's comedian, constantly joking with staff and other kids. She even predicted that one day I would appear on *The Arsenio Hall Show*, a popular talk show at the time. This revelation surprised my mother, as at home, I was often quiet, engrossed in watching TV and playing video games. It was at daycare where my extroverted side shone first, unbeknownst to my family. This outgoing nature was mirrored in my adult life. My bold fashion choices and perfectly manicured nails are outward expressions of my vibrant personality, and I pride myself on being authentic and disarming before greeting teachers. So, when the pandemic forced

DOI: 10.4324/9781003404163-4

a shift to remote work, it eliminated my ability to employ my usual outgoing expressions as tools to connect with the audience.

As the pandemic continued, my workshops started to feel more transactional and less engaging. While functional, webinars and virtual sessions seemed to create barriers I struggled to overcome. It was challenging to gauge the teachers' reactions and adjust my approach accordingly, something I could easily do in a face-to-face setting. The spontaneity and dynamic interplay of in-person interactions were replaced by a more structured, less personal format. This shift was particularly hard for me as someone who thrived on direct, personal connections. The remote setting also limited my ability to use physical cues and body language effectively. The energy and enthusiasm I could convey through my presence in a room were now confined to the small window of a computer screen. This new environment required a different set of skills and adaptations that I couldn't seem to learn quickly enough. But I knew something had to change. I needed to connect with teachers somehow.

One day, while decluttering my at-home teaching space, I started swapping furnishings and books from other rooms in the home. Eventually decluttering turned into shopping on Amazon, and a week later, I completely revamped my home office. Throughout the spontaneous revamping, I focused on creating a space that not only functioned well for work but also reflected my personality and style. I chose a vibrant color scheme that energized the room, painting the walls a shade of orangish pink named "Persimmon" as the backdrop for my video calls. I replaced my standard office chair with a more comfortable, stylish one, ensuring long work hours were less taxing on my back. I strategically placed a few personal items, like framed photos and a small collection of my favorite books on a shelf within the camera's view, adding a personal touch to the space. Additionally, I invested in a better webcam and microphone, improving the audio-visual quality of my presentations. This redesign transformed my home office into a space that was not just a place to work, but a space that I was proud to teach in, just like my classroom.

So, it was a no-brainer that I would turn off the blur image filter the day after I finished setting up my new and improved home teaching setup. In the first training of the day, my usual opening, a cheerful "Hey loves, how are y'all today?" rang out at the start, and the chat exploded; several teachers were buzzing with questions, not about how they were doing, but with a chorus of "Where'd you get that lamp?" I blinked, then grinned. My spontaneous design choices, driven by a need to boost my own spirits, had unexpectedly become a conversation starter. That lamp, a charming transplant from another room, had sparked a shared love of aesthetics, a human connection across the digital divide. Embracing the moment, I launched into a lighthearted rant about my inner shopaholic and confessed the lamp's humble origins. I promised to share my favorite budget-friendly home decor haunts after the session, then, with a playful wink, offered: "Anyone wanna snap a picture of my room and google image search items that you wanna buy?"

As I continued with the training session, I noticed a shift in the energy of the group. The initial stiffness and formality had given way to a more relaxed and open exchange of ideas. My personal story about the lamp had broken down some barriers and created a shared sense of camaraderie among us. It was as if my vulnerability had given permission for others to be themselves and open up as well. I was reminded that training teachers is never solely about conveying information; it's also about connecting with people on a human level. In the remaining sessions of the day, more teachers ranted about my digs, and in an effort to weave in more personal anecdotes and encourage others to share their own, I leaned into it. I felt like my extroverted self again for the first time since the pandemic started. By the end of the day, I felt like I had made some genuine connections with my audience, even though we were all miles apart and communicating through screens. That day was one of many reminders that even in this digital age, human connection is still possible.

During the COVID-19 pandemic, my background became a secret weapon to bridge the connection gap between teachers and myself. By displaying little sparks of my personality, my home office transformed from a mere backdrop into an extension of myself. It became a new tool for fostering a community of learning that pulsed with the warmth of human interaction. All it took was a decluttering spree, a dash of orangish pink, and the courage to let my lamp do the talking.

Lesson Learned: Your Webcam Background is an Essential Part of Your Virtual Presentation Style, so Choose it Wisely

Unfortunately, presenting virtually won't give you the chance to showcase your new shoes or congratulate someone with a high five for their excellent contribution. However, there are other ways to shine and engage with the audience when you're teaching online. You should think like a pioneer, finding innovative ways to adapt the methods that work in-person to an online format that requires internet access and video conferencing services. This also means you may have to become more tech-savvy and rely less on the IT department to manage your passwords and computer settings. But just like you're (mostly) unphased when you move classrooms or present in varying spaces, you must be confident in entering and adapting to new, online environments. You got this. No more fear of seeing yourself on camera because Chapter 4 will enhance your confidence as a virtual presenter by translating the good habits mentioned in Chapters 1–3.

Optimizing Your Virtual Presentation Space

Presenting virtually presents unique challenges that are not encountered during in-person training. One of the most significant differences is the need for microphones. When giving a presentation online, it's crucial to speak clearly and utilize a microphone to ensure everyone can hear you, especially if you're presenting to a large group of people. While giving a presentation in person, you can typically speak freely without worrying about whether or not you're being heard. Additionally, when you're in person, you can rely less on visual aids and more on your movements and body language. But when you're virtual, you're usually confined to the engagement that occurs within the frame of your camera lens. That's why it's crucial to master the key components of the online teaching space that allow you to teach with the same enthusiasm you're used to when you meet someone in person. To assist you in creating a setup that emphasizes teacher interaction, Table 4.1 presents a virtual presentation checklist that aligns with adult learning best practices.

TABLE 4.1 Checklist for optimizing virtual presentation spaces with justifications

Essential Question	Why it Matters	Checklist
How will your audience see you?	Teachers relate more to presenters who feel familiar and who have "walked the walk." An easy way to show your relatability is to show yourself… on camera.	◆ Make sure your built-in or attached webcam functions by logging into your web meeting software app and confirm clear video output. ◆ Are you satisfied with your background and appearance? Do you need to source lighting or use a virtual background?
How will your audience see the content you present?	In order to connect with the adult learner, you must be able to demonstrate the practicality of your content; this often requires you to use visuals, such as video clips.	◆ Practice using the screen share feature of your web meeting software.
How will your audience hear you?	Adults are easily distracted by many high-priority responsibilities, so if for some reason someone can't watch you, they can rely on your authentic tone.	◆ Log in to your web meeting app to ensure your microphone works properly.
How will you interact with the audience?	Adults thrive when they're able to make personal connections with the presenter, so prioritize the way you plan to execute interaction.	◆ Locate and practice using the Chat function of your web meeting app. ◆ Practice copying and pasting information to participants. ◆ (If applicable) Locate and practice using the web meeting app's polling features.
How will you toggle between presenting content and interacting with participants?	Adults have very short attention spans, so it's important to maneuver through content smoothly.	◆ Know how to drag and resize different programs on your computer. ◆ Know how to rearrange, drag, and resize different tabs in your web browser. ◆ Practice your computer's split screen. ◆ Determine if you have enough space to engage with your audience and present your content. Consider a dual monitor setup if you need more visual space.

The Importance of Signposting

When I'm in person, I rarely present norms or plan time for housekeeping tasks because I typically instruct in places where teachers know the Wi-Fi password and where the bathrooms are located. In virtual spaces, however, presenting behavioral norms and signposting where to click and when are essential discussion topics. If you plan to engage with teachers during your presentation, be clear about how to do so because you can't assume they're as savvy as you are with the capabilities of the web meeting platform. For example, if someone wants to provide verbal feedback, that person must know how to use the mute/unmute feature. If someone prefers to respond in the chat, they'll need to know where the chat function is. And if the person is like me and prefers to multi-task with the web content and digital notes loaded side by side, then they need to know how to swiftly travel across windows and tabs. So, if you have a particular engagement feature, habit, or process you want to use throughout your presentation, underscore that information in a quick housekeeping chat after your initial greeting and when you call for participation. Below are the top five things I signpost during virtual presentations.

1. How do teachers raise their hands to get your attention?
2. How do teachers chat with you? With the rest of the group?
3. How can teachers quickly react or respond to your ad hoc questions?
4. How can teachers take the lead by unmuting and presenting their screens?
5. How can teachers multitask by rearranging the video content of your presentation with their own open applications?

 Transferable Teacher Tip #10: Get to the Class Early

It's always wise to arrive in your classroom with ample time to prepare the room for learners, and the same applies to your virtual classroom. Allow ample time before your sessions to make sure all of the virtual setup components are in place and functioning properly.

Beaming and Building Rapport through the Webcam

Beaming with an authentic smile comes naturally when you're face to face with others because oftentimes they smile back at you. On the computer, however, there could be times when you're the only person on camera, beaming back at yourself. Even worse, you may be one of many trainers who loathe seeing themselves on camera. Whether it's poor lighting or a lack of confidence living in the camera lens, even I, a self-proclaimed lover of being on camera, am rarely satisfied with how I look on screen. This tendency for us to dislike the way we look on camera is a form of confirmation bias. Encyclopedia Britannica defines this as "people's tendency to process information by looking for, or interpreting, information that is consistent with their existing beliefs." Essentially, because we often go into virtual presentations with a propensity to dislike how we look on camera, we're more likely to lean into the idea that we'll look bad regardless of lighting, filters, or outfits. Britannica goes on to share that "this biased approach to decision making is largely unintentional, and it results in a person ignoring information that is inconsistent with their beliefs" (Casad & Luebering, 2016). So, how can a virtual presenter beam and build rapport with confidence? We must offer alternatives to our consideration bias.

Self-Affirming Thoughts to Counter Your Confirmation Bias

◆ "I'm a wizard at connecting with people. I'm gonna make so many new relationships during my training that it won't matter what I look like."

◆ "I'm competent and confident in what I'm presenting; people will see that no matter what."

◆ "My value is determined by my passion and resonance with teachers, not by the way I look."

◆ "Every time I present virtually, my skillset grows along with my confidence on camera."

◆ "I focus on relevance and rapport when I present; that will always trump physical appearance."

Transferable Teacher Tip #11: Dress for Success

Just because you'll be presenting on camera, that doesn't mean that your attire won't impact training outcomes. Similar to the way your in-person teaching wardrobe is professional with components of personality, so should the outfits you wear on camera. In most cases, your upper body will be the only part of you visible on camera, so take extra care choosing what you wear from the waist up.

Insights from a Learning Design Expert: Marc Dembowski

Marc Dembowski, Senior Learning Designer at AVID Center, highlighted the value of intentional backgrounds, along with other insights, in an interview I conducted with him in 2023. In our 1:1 chat, Dembowski highlighted the importance of authenticity and personalization in virtual sessions. He advocated in favor of using real backgrounds to create a more genuine and relatable environment that facilitates natural conversations and connections. While pointing to a blanket hanging on his wall, Marc proclaimed, "It's like what I have done here. I have a blanket hanging on my wall behind me. It's my alma mater, the University of Arizona…it allows for natural conversations to take place like where I went to college." Marc's approach not only makes sessions more relatable but also helps in building trust and rapport with participants. In essence, Dembowski's insights underscore the importance of seeking new opportunities to make personal connections with virtual audiences.

Marc also offered valuable guidance on becoming an effective virtual presenter by adapting in-person teaching strategies to the virtual environment, emphasizing the importance of chunking learning. He stated,

> We should be chunking online learning. Just like we would not lecture or conduct a 'sit and get' in person for an hour. Think…How are you going to break the learning up so that it is manageable to digest and engaging?

This approach is crucial for maintaining engagement and facilitating information retention, particularly vital in a digital setting where attention spans can be more limited.

Lastly, Marc emphasized that building relational capacity was an essential component of all presentations, especially virtual ones. Dembowski underscored the significance of interactive and movement-based activities, even in an online format, to break monotony and keep participants engaged. He mentioned, "Energizers and state changers… are a must in all of our PD regardless of if it's in person or online." His strategy not only aids in keeping the session lively but also contributes to a more dynamic and participatory learning experience. With the help of built-in polling and collaborative whiteboards, virtual presentation tools like Zoom and Google Meet offer the ability to boost energy and relatability with a few clicks (Dembowski, personal communication, November 13, 2023).

 Transferable Teacher Tip #12: Use Technology to Visualize Real-Time Responses

In the classroom, teachers ask students ad hoc questions in every lesson. Keep this effective strategy to check for understanding in your virtual workshops by using the web meeting chat or polling add-on to quickly gather audience feedback.

Learning to Love the Sound of Your Voice

D2L, a learning management system and education services provider, published a survey report entitled "How the Pandemic has (Re)Shaped K–12 Teacher Professional Learning" that underscores the increasing demand for online, asynchronous teacher professional learning (Schneiderman, 2022). In its survey of 127 school administrators and 850 teachers, 55% of teachers said their interest in online, on-demand professional learning had increased since before the pandemic. This, along with an overall increase in learning management system use, indicates that teacher trainers will be increasingly asked to deliver presentations in an asynchronous format. As a result, we can expect to create more recorded versions of our trainings, which usually require re-watching and editing before publishing. I have to admit that I used to dread this. When I started creating recorded presentations during my graduate school experience in 2017, I was quite insecure. I would often re-record presentations so that I would sound more masculine since I didn't like the sound of my voice. One day, when I was pressed for time and late turning in an assignment, I recorded a presentation in one take without any edits. I couldn't watch it back because I was afraid I would cringe. Surprisingly, after I turned in the recording, my professor appreciated my inflection and authenticity. That was the beginning of me learning to embrace the sassy, slightly effeminate sound of my voice. Seven years later, I've accepted who I am, and I love my sassy, slightly effeminate intonation because it makes me unique. It's another aspect that allows me to connect with the audience by being myself and not putting on a facade. To help you love the sound of your voice, I've included a few of my top strategies:

- ◆ Go out to Karaoke Night. Belting it out on the microphone will help normalize hearing your voice back.
- ◆ Watch your presentations back without looking at the screen so that you become more familiar with the sound of your voice.
- ◆ Deliver a presentation to a friend using no visuals. Focus on being relaxed and casual.
- ◆ Record your voice during in-person training and compare that with the voice you use in asynchronous training. Try to replicate whichever is the most authentic.

Putting it into Action

Reflect	Explore	Experiment
The next time you get an opportunity to watch someone else present virtually, write down all of the visual elements you love. What about these visual elements that made you love them?	Virtual presentation tools are constantly evolving. To become more familiar with the software you use for virtual presentations, search YouTube for tutorials, tips, and tricks.	Include personal artifacts or wear your favorite outfit in your next virtual training. Naturally embed them as talking points to share more about who you are as a person. Document how this made you feel and how the audience reacted.

References

Casad, B. J., & Luebering, J. E. (2016). Confirmation Bias. In Encyclopedia Britannica.https://www.britannica.com/science/confirmation-bias

Dembowski, M. (2023, November 13). [Interview by M. Stein].

Schneiderman, M. (2022). How the Pandemic has (Re)Shaped K–12 Teacher Professional Learning: Survey Findings, Research Brief and Recommendations. https://www.d2l.com/resources/assets/ways-to-support-teachers-professional-development/?asset=7015W00 00009bpSQAQ

5

Professional Growth

In the Fall of 2016, I started hearing about Edcamp NOLA among my professional learning network (PLN), and I planned to attend (it was FREE after all). This Saturday, professional development event was pitched as the "anti-conference" where the topics were not chosen beforehand. The participants would come together in person and build topics and discussion leaders based on the needs and interests of the small group of in-person attendees. I loved the idea of being able to personalize a teacher meetup on the fly, so I registered.

But when I noticed one of my EdTech friends, Valerie Burton, posting about organizing the event with a planning committee, I reached out to her and expressed interest in helping. I had never helped plan a professional development event, and I was eager to gain some experience in pulling off a PD opportunity of this scale. Valerie quickly said yes to my volunteer offer, and we started preparing for the event two months before the event's scheduled date of October 26, 2016.

The 2016 Edcamp NOLA planning committee was like the *X-Men* – a gang of superteachers all with unique backgrounds and expertise – oftentimes stifled by the confines of our daytime duties. Some of the members were full-time professional development consultants, some were coaches and technology leaders, and others were incredibly passionate classroom teachers.

Because the design of Edcamp NOLA was NOT to plan topics or the schedule ahead of time, we spent most of our preparation

DOI: 10.4324/9781003404163-5

planning how we would facilitate the discussion of topics and topic leaders. And after securing a school to host the event, we scheduled a day to walk the campus and map out how we wanted the event to run. We chose a central commons area to gather for all-group conversations and then six of the nearest classrooms as breakout spaces. We also picked a spot near the entrance for registration and dispersed snacks and refreshments throughout the common area. Little did I know that during that walkthrough, I would meet my PLN confidant. My most trustworthy peer who would always remind me that a great teacher leader is always polishing.

During that walkthrough, I immediately gravitated to Tinashe Blanchet. At the time, she was a Google Certified Trainer and national presenter for the Bureau of Education Research. She and I both lived in New Orleans, and we both worked full-time as education consultants. As I traversed the halls of our Edcamp NOLA host school, I thought to myself "THIS woman is going places. I want to know her. She's smart and funny and authentic like me. I want to be her friend." So when the school walkthrough commenced, Tinashe and I exchanged phone numbers; and within an hour of that, we were already chatting on the phone about what we planned to wear to the upcoming PD event.

Somewhere in the midst of our conversation, Tinashe mentioned that one of her mentors had recently honed in on helping to polish her presentation style. And as she talked about being polished by her mentor, I thought to myself, "This woman IS polished. I've seen her in action on the Edcamp NOLA planning committee. I've heard from many of my peers that she's a brilliant presenter. I've Googled her. She seems quite polished." But according to her, this particular mentor and his polishing tips were the reason why her presentations were becoming more and more effective and engaging. Tinashe then added, "It's been really helpful. In fact, I want to help polish you, Marcus." Without thinking, I blurted, "I don't need polishing. My presentation style is already fun, engaging, and authentic. What I really need is more experience and opportunities. That's all." I was offended by Tinashe's offer to polish me. My mind started to race with questions like: Do I not appear polished already? How could a peer (someone doing the same work as me) polish me? Does Tinashe think I'm looking for a mentor in her? Her expertise and mine are totally different, so how could she possibly teach me how to be a better presenter? And Tinashe sensed my defensiveness immediately, so being a cool, calm mother of three, she wrapped up the conversation with a friendly "let's revisit this later." We agreed to disagree and decided to chat about it sometime in the future.

By October 26, 2016, the date of the annual Edcamp NOLA conference, Tinashe and I had become fast friends who frequently exchanged notes about our favorite happy hour spots in New Orleans; of course we would chat about our work lives, but at the core of our relationship was an ever-growing sense of trust and respect. Hence why Tinashe and I worked incredibly well together facilitating conversations at Edcamp NOLA 2016. She and I freely exchanged giving and receiving orders throughout the day without ever questioning "Who's in charge here?" And after a successful day of fellowship with 20ish local New Orleans educators, the committee members had a quick debriefing, packed up our resources, and then reset the school to its usual arrangement. Tinashe and I had our own debriefing on the phone as we drove home that afternoon.

> That was so fun! I want to do more work planning professional development events, but it's so hard to get opportunities like this. Conference planning boards and committees are usually limited. And those limited spots are usually voted on. And oftentimes there are politics involved with these roles. Why is it so difficult to offer my FREE help on these planning committees?

Tinashe replied,

> Well, it's all in how you frame what you want and where you want to be. It sounds like you're thinking about your future from a scarcity mindset. You're maneuvering as if there are a finite amount of positions for someone wanting what you want. If you thought with an abundance mindset, you'd be way less concerned about what

other people are doing and much more focused on being a better teacher leader.

And that is when something clicked in my brain. I don't remember how long I paused after Tinashe made this statement, but in that brief "ah ha" moment, I realized how much potential knowledge, growth, and opportunity I had been missing out on; I was so focused on being greater than every other teacher leader that I was missing out on moments like the one I was having with my friend – moments where I'm so open and trusting of my surroundings so that I'm able to receive growth at anytime. Tinashe's words helped me to start envision flipping my mindset to one of abundance. I thought to myself,

> How would I behave if there were an infinite amount of spaces for me to be the leader I want to be? What if there weren't any competition for teacher leader positions? Would I then care who offered to help polish me? Would I be more inclined to help support teacher leaders?

After my awkward prolonged silence, I spoke up, "You know what, friend?" I said.

> You are so right. In fact, that competitive, scarcity mindset might be the reason why I was so unwilling to accept your offer to help polish me. I was offended because I looked at you as a competitor trying to occupy the same space as me. When in reality, you're trying to be a useful source of professional growth for me. I'm sorry about my initial reaction. I'd love to learn from you anytime. Polish away.

Lesson Learned: Adopting an Abundance Mindset Shifts Your Focus from Peers to Self-Improvement

In his best-selling book *The 7 Habits of Highly Effective People*, Stephen R. Covey (2020), a self-help and business thought leader, compares and contrasts the scarcity and abundance mindsets.

Those with scarcity mindsets "see life as having only so much, as though there were only one pie out there. And if someone were to get a big piece of the pie, it would mean less for everybody else" (p. 250). It was the scarcity mindset that there's a finite amount of learning sources and opportunities that almost cost me a lifelong friendship and polishing source in Tinashe. In contrast, an abundance mindset "is the paradigm that there is plenty out there and enough to spare for everybody" (p. 251). Shifting to this mentality allowed me to be open to learning beyond the sources I initially deemed worthy. And ultimately, thinking abundantly has been the accelerator for my personal and professional growth.

Thinking of Professional Growth with Abundance

Teachable moments can happen anytime, anywhere, but if we're not open to noticing and learning from these moments, we're only stifling our growth. This is one of the hardest professional growth strategies to adopt because we tend to see less experienced educators or those who haven't "walked the walk" as less valuable sources of growth. We then seek our knowledge by creating ambitious growth plans without room for spontaneous or unexpected learning. And we pick and choose when and where to upskill rather than accepting that a polishing moment can happen even when we're not looking for it. To receive a wider array of teachable moments, we must replace some of our scarcity mindset growth habits (Table 5.1).

Mentorship through the Lens of Abundance

Without any connotation, a mentor is typically thought of as an experienced advisor chosen to lead a younger, less experienced person. Unfortunately, taking this definition at face value can lead to a narrowed, scarce sourcing of mentorship. For instance, if you only seek older mentors, you risk missing out on learning opportunities from highly experienced, younger mentors. Also, if your mentorship definition is narrowed by experience levels only, you're stifling your mentor options due to the ambiguous nature of the word "experience." Essentially, the traditional definition of a mentor restricts the size of the mentorship pool to those who have "won" or have "made it to the top." With an abundance mindset, though, you think less competitively and are more open to focusing on the traits and habits you want to learn

TABLE 5.1 Tips for planning professional growth with an abundance mindset

Instead of Thinking with Scarcity by…	Try Thinking with Abundance and…
Creating a full-year professional growth plan filled with workshops and conferences that take advantage of 100% of your available learning time	Plan informal meetups with your peers with the intention of talking less and listening more
Making Graduate School coursework your primary source of professional growth	Get to know your classmates and peers and their expertise
Building a Professional Learning Network of all "yes" people	Befriend and add peers to your PLN who have contrasting opinions and points of view
Aiming to be an expert in a specific topic or role	Finding more opportunities to learn where you are a novice
Attending a teacher conference mainly as a presenter	Lead fewer workshops than you attend with the intent of learning more than you teach
Improving content knowledge only	Balance your professional growth with content knowledge and andragogy

from a mentor. Therefore, the first step toward growing professionally through mentorship is to reimagine the definition of the word mentor. And once you begin identifying potential mentors based on the actual traits and habits you want to grow, you must also secure and maintain mentorships with a continued abundance mindset. In her Indeed.com blog "How to Find a Mentor in 8 Steps," Jennifer Herrity suggests that the best way to secure a new mentor is to create an elevator pitch that succinctly shares "why you think this person is the right mentor for you, and your expectations of them confidently." After mastering your pitch and gaining initial interest from mentors, Herrity provides some advice on maintaining mentor relationships:

Set a goal. Having a goal for your mentorship helps focus your relationship. Decide what you want to achieve, and develop a plan with your mentor about how to do it.

Form a personal relationship. A good personal relationship with your mentor is important for fostering a good mentoring relationship with them. Familiarize yourself with them, and make it a priority to work well with them.

Accept constructive criticism. Constructive feedback is crucial for fostering your professional growth. Learn how to accept constructive criticism from your mentor, and apply it to improve your career.

Practice gratitude. Being a mentor is often a significant commitment. Thank them for their guidance in ways like giving them handwritten thank-you notes after each section or providing a professional recommendation for them (Herrity, 2023).

Diversify the Feedback You Absorb

As mentioned in Chapter 2, a significant component that will drive the effectiveness of your presentations is direct feedback from the teachers you lead, but this isn't the only source of feedback that can direct your professional growth. The University of California Santa Barbara's Instructional Department provides feedback ideas beyond your post-training feedback survey by emphasizing self-reflection, peer feedback, and measurable participant outcomes (UCSB, n.d.).

Self-Reflection

When was the last time you questioned the effectiveness and the engagement levels of your professional development workshops? Compared and contrasted with the critiques of your attendees, your own reflections can help affirm your presentation choices and highlight ineffective practices. The formality of this process is up to you, but the Instructional Department at US Santa Barbara suggests journaling the essentials: thoughts, questions, and ideas before and after your trainings. The format and medium of your journal are irrelevant, but in order to make journaling a natural component of your professional growth, I suggest housing your self-reflections in the most convenient location for you. A paper notebook, an online doc, or an app on your phone will all suffice. In your journal, It is also suggested that you link to presentations and planning materials and then annotate the parts that were and weren't effective. This will help you remember when and where things worked and didn't work. If you're having trouble starting your reflection journey or if you ever veer into a space of over-critiquing yourself, focus on affirmations. Ask yourself, "What am I doing well?"

Transferable Teacher Tip #13: Reflect During Your Commute

On your commute, your mind is already teeming with thoughts of work, so make this time intentional. Spend a few minutes of this time affirming yourself by thinking of the positive practices you've exhibited recently.

Peer Feedback

Presenting in front of other presenters is another valuable form of feedback; however, if you don't seek out opportunities to convene with other presenters, you may never be able to take advantage of this valuable perspective. So, how does one get feedback from other presenters if most of your time is spent with teachers? Simply stated: attend more conferences and teacher meetups. In-person conferences provide opportunities for networking and building relationships with other educators who share your passion for improving education. Realistically, though, conferences can often be costly or require time away from the teachers you support. So, if the cost and logistical commitment of in-person conferences is a barrier, I suggest two things: search and sign up for your nearest Edcamp and harness the human connections made possible through social media.

Digital Promise provides the best summary of the Edcamp experience by proclaiming that "Edcamps are free public events that leverage the knowledge and experiences of attendees by allowing educators to collaboratively determine topics for discussion the day of the event" (Edcamp Community, 2020). And that's exactly what it was like for me when I attended my local Edcamp: a complimentary meeting of the minds and another place to gather feedback from others on the same journey as you. This space provides a free opportunity for you to lead discussions, absorb information from others, and collect feedback from a group of passionate educators with the same fervor for lifelong learning as you.

Unlike the annual or biannual structure of Edcamps, social media can inform and guide your PD delivery style anytime and anywhere. Because social media platforms are dominated by influencers and trends, though, you may not initially envision the feedback opportunity these apps can provide. A 2020 article titled "Using Social Media for Teacher Professional Development" provides insights into navigating the business of apps like X (formerly Twitter), Facebook, and Instagram.

1. First, remember your goal; you're seeking peer feedback, so ignore follower counts and likes, and focus on finding the hashtag or group of threads that help grow your practice.
2. Once you identify meaningful users and hashtags, follow and bookmark them.
3. When you're ready for feedback, post and ask for engagement from others by including the hashtag or by mentioning identified followers (Friedman, 2020). Not sure which hashtags to include? Use them all. A mixture of broad and specific hashtags allows you to source and participate in a wider variety of conversations (Table 5.2).

 Transferable Teacher Tip #14: Share Your Work Online

You already use social media to consume the information you're looking for, so spend some of that online time looking for growth through peer feedback. Share work and ideas online and request feedback from your peers. If you're brave enough to post a selfie, you're brave enough to share your expertise.

Measurable Participant Outcomes

In the classroom, the teacher's impact can be partially gauged based on student assessment results and behaviors across a semester or school year. The teacher can use that assessment data as feedback to improve future lessons. But with professional development, there is no standardized test or behavioral standard to measure teacher progress, so it can be difficult and

TABLE 5.2 Popular broad and specific social media hashtags to use when seeking peer feedback

#TeacherPD	Broad	Use this hashtag to share your original PD and source inspiration from other presenters
#EdLeadership #TeacherLeadership #EduCoach	Broad	Use these hashtags for anything encompassing education leadership
#EdChat	Broad	Use this hashtag to join and participate in ongoing conversations about current issues in education
#_____Teacher	Specific	Include a subject area before the word "Teacher" to create a hashtag targeting a specific subject focus (i.e., #MathTeacher, Science Teacher, etc.)
#EdTech	Specific	Use this hashtag to indicate your connection to instructional technology

time-consuming to determine the measurable impacts of your trainings. That doesn't mean teacher-trainee metrics don't exist. With the help of supervisor polling, observation, and software analytics, it is possible to get pre- and post-assessment data on your audience members to partially inform your effectiveness levels (Table 5.3).

TABLE 5.3 Guide for gathering measurable training data using supervisor polling, observation, and software analytics

	Step 1: Pre-Assessment	Step 2: Post-Assessment	Step 3: Measurable Outcomes
Supervisor Polling	Ask a supervisor to rate your audience's prowess with the topic or skill you plan to teach.	A month after your workshop ends, ask the supervisor to re-rate the teachers.	Are multiple stakeholders citing positive or negative changes in teacher behaviors after your training?
Observation	Choose an observable behavior, monitor participants before your instruction, and create a baseline for your audience.	At determined intervals after the training, re-observe audience members.	Are there any changes in observable behaviors as a result of your training?
Software Analytics	If you're teaching a topic of skill that requires a software program, ask the school IT department for a usage report.	A month after the workshop ends, ask for the same usage data again.	After your training, do usage reports indicate that teachers implementing the software with more or less fidelity?

You've Got All This Feedback, Now What?

If you genuinely absorb all sources of feedback, you'll be quickly inundated with critiques and may not know how to interpret and action it all. The University of California Santa Barbara provides a few suggestions on how to filter and decode the mountain of feedback that builds throughout your career.

1. **Think about what matters most to you when combing through feedback.** Are you improving your grasp of the content? Are you improving your public speaking skills? Are you building confidence with your virtual presentation style? If you ask these questions before going swimming in your ocean of feedback, you'll be able to collate and filter quickly.
2. **Scan your feedback and look for trends and outliers.** This will prevent the "loudest" feedback from dominating your growth strategy. If you find this skimming and scanning tedious, try using an AI tool like ChapGPT to find trends in your digital feedback.
3. **Have a place to store the changes you want to make to your teaching.** Consuming and reflecting on your practices should lead to some form of action, and to ensure that you follow through on your intended actions, create a growth repository of things you want to change or experiment with as a presenter. Choose a system you can search and access anywhere like the cloud-based notes on your phone or within a cloud storage system like Google Drive or OneDrive. My growth repository has changed format throughout the years, and sometimes I prefer to use a word processing app as opposed to an annotation app, but I've been keeping it all in the

---

 Transferable Teacher Tip #15: Organize Your Learnings

Teachers store and organize instructional materials so that they can easily be sourced and implemented based on the needs of the students. Think of your professional growth materials the same way. Take a moment to make sure you can easily locate, skim, and scan your personal library of teachable trainer moments.

same cloud storage location since I started presenting to teachers (Documenting Teaching, n.d.).

Upskilling Your Soft Skills

It's a given that we must maintain a firm grasp of our teacher-leader content knowledge. And for many of us, continued education is mandatory and embedded into our job roles. However, to sustain long-term effectiveness, we must learn nontechnical, behavioral skills often learned outside our job duties. These personality-centric skills that improve your work performance by improving thoughts and habits are called soft skills.

As job demands evolve, so will the soft skills required to flourish in the workplace. It is because of this that soft skill development can sometimes feel like an endless, unattainable endeavor. The World Economic Forum, however, provides some insight into the most consistent soft skills that accelerate professional growth in its annual "The Future of Jobs Report." After interviewing over 803 companies across 27 industries worldwide, two soft skills surfaced as the most in-demand in the past, present, and future of professional growth: creative thinking and analytical thinking (World Economic Forum, 2023).

Becoming a creative thinker, however, can be difficult as a Teacher Trainer, especially when you're tasked with delivering the same content repeatedly. Creative thinking can be stifled further when teaching mandatory, scripted workshops. But when things go awry, and adaptations are needed, the creative brain is the one that can think out of the box and provide a wider variety of solutions. Analytical thinking, the ability to break down and solve complex issues, goes hand in hand with creativity. Being an adept analytical Teacher Trainer gives you the ability to better take a bird's eye view of the populations you work with; it also takes the fear out of designing scale-able professional development workshops because you're able to work more logically with all stakeholders involved. Thus, the consistent evolution of your innovation expertise and your logic skills are essential to professional growth. But if your entire day is devoted to supporting teachers, when and where do you find the time to exercise your creative and analytical muscles?

1. **Think without limits.** When your job presents challenges, ignore barriers, both tangible and intangible. This will feel and sound incredulous, especially if you're working alongside others. However, if you start your creative process as if time, money, or skill aren't a hurdle, then the most excessive, outlandish ideas will surface first. Write or make mental notes of them all. This will allow you to sift through and source attainable parts of your crazy ideas that can become components of a newfound, creative vision.

2. **Invest in a Thinkpak.** Invented by creativity expert Michael Michalko, the Thinkpak is a deck of cards that challenges your ideas by shuffling through the SCAMPER method. By shuffling and dealing with these cards, your thoughts will be challenged in seven ways: Substitution, Combination, Adaptation, Modification, Putting to Another Use, Elimination, and Reversal. The cards also include real-world examples of how major industries have implemented these methods to solve some of their largest problems (Michalko, 2006). I keep a deck of Thinkpak cards in my laptop bag for anytime my brain gets stuck, or anytime I need inspiration for an impromptu brainstorming session.

3. **Take advantage of free, online courses.** Thinking without limits and using a Thinkpack can both be performed as problems arise, without having to devote much energy outside of the workday. However, if you do find yourself upskilling outside of work, try growing your creativity and analysis skills via free online courses like the Applied Digital Skills that Google hosts. These free activities are designed to directly grow your hard skills like business writing and budgeting while simultaneously boosting your creative and analytical skills through project-based lessons. Browse the lessons and activities via applieddigitalskills.withgoogle.com (Google Applied Digital Skills - Teach & Learn Practical Digital Skills, 2017).

Never Stop Growing

An abundance mindset is a powerful tool for personal growth and development. When you adopt an abundance mindset, you believe that there are unlimited possibilities available to you. This mindset encourages you to think big, take risks, and seek out new opportunities.

One of the major benefits of having an abundance mindset is the natural inclination to grow continuously. When you believe that there is always room for growth and improvement, you'll be more open to new ideas and sources of information. This can help you absorb new skills, both intentionally and unintentionally. To foster this growth mindset, it's important to actively seek out new mentors and sources of feedback. These individuals can offer valuable insights and guidance that can help you achieve your goals. Additionally, it's important to work on developing your soft skills, such as creative and analytical thinking. By embracing an abundance mindset, you'll be able to approach challenges with a positive outlook and see each obstacle as an opportunity for growth and learning.

Putting it into Action

Reflect	Explore	Experiment
Take a journey to your future self, ten years from now. What creative teaching practices have become your trademark? What insights or advice does your future self offer regarding cultivating creative thinking skills?	Use Table 5.2 to perform a refined social media search for conversations about soft skills beyond creative and analytical thinking. How many new soft skills upskilling sources can you identify?	Volunteer to serve on the planning committee of the next education conference or meeting you plan to attend. Use this as an opportunity to fellowship with peers and unearth new potential mentors.

References

Covey, S. R. (2020). The 7 habits of highly effective people: 30Th anniversary edition (30th ed.). Simon & Schuster.

Documenting Teaching. (n.d.). UCSB.edu. Retrieved December 4, 2023, from https://id.ucsb.edu/teaching/teaching-resources/evaluating-teaching/documenting-teaching

Edcamp Community. (2020, May 21). Digital Promise. https://digital promise.org/edcamp/

Friedman, J. (2020, January 16). Using Social Media for Teacher Professional Development. Hmhco.com.https://www.hmhco.com/blog/using-social-media-for-teacher-professional-development

Google Applied Digital Skills - Teach & Learn Practical Digital Skills. (2017). Withgoogle.com. https://applieddigitalskills.withgoogle.com/s/en/home

Herrity, J. (2023, February 3). How to Find a Mentor in 8 Steps. Indeed Career Guide. https://www.indeed.com/career-advice/career-development/how-to-find-a-mentor

Michalko, M. (2006). Thinkpak. Ten Speed Press.

UCSB (n.d.). Sources of Feedback. Retrieved December 4, 2023, from https://id.ucsb.edu/teaching/teaching-resources/evaluating-teaching/sources-of-feedback

World Economic Forum. (2023). The Future of Jobs Report 2023. World Economic Forum. https://www.weforum.org/publications/the-future-of-jobs-report-2023/

Conclusion

When she joined the Zoom meeting, my eyes immediately centered on her headset because she looked like a telemarking call center worker, not the bubbly, dynamic presenter I hired. "What's with the headset?" I blurted without hesitation. "We provided you with a new MacBook, a 4k webcam, and a podcast-quality microphone, so do you need the headset because you live in a noisy, distracting environment?" Melissa replied, "No, I have a dedicated space in my house for virtual meetings and presentations. I've just always been told that the headset is the most professional way to host online meetups." I chuckled and responded, "Let me ask you this. When you work with teachers, is it your professionalism that they resonate with or your bright, relatable, and passionate instructional expertise?" She paused and then declared, "I've always worn the headset when I teach online, so I just prefer it." Before shifting the conversation to a discussion about her onboarding at Kami, I said, "It's all good, Melissa. I want you to do whatever makes you feel confident."

I met Melissa Summerford, a former elementary teacher and professional development consultant, at the TCEA (Texas Computer Education Association) conference in February of 2022. I was accepted to deliver a Kami-sponsored presentation at the conference, and Melissa was paired with me as a conference representative. The only interaction we had prior to the in-person event was a few brief email exchanges where we solidified our slides and presentation outline. When I walked into the ballroom half an hour before our presentation start time, I noticed her from across the room. Donning sequin pants, black velvet boots, and bright yellow earrings, I was immediately impressed by her fashion sense. And when I walked up to her, and she greeted me with a loving smile and hug, I knew that she and I were kindred spirits. Before we could connect our computers and set up for the

DOI: 10.4324/9781003404163-6

presentation, she pulled out her phone and said, "We look cute. Let's take some pics." She didn't know this at the time, but I'm a lover of selfies, so I dropped all of my belongings and leaped into model mode. At one point, we had to ask the room moderator to snap our photo so we could capture our full, flashy ensembles. When attendees started to pour into the room, Melissa beat me to the greeting. She was the first to smile and say hello to everyone who entered, and we had no trouble building immediate rapport by disarming the entire room. Once the presentation started, Melissa and I initially followed our choreographed script, but shortly into it, she and I both pointed the microphone at the audience, allowing them to lead with their own questions and expertise. And by the end of the session, it felt like I made a new friend in both Melissa and the 100+ teachers in the audience.

Hence, when I had the opportunity to hire a new Teacher Success Champion at Kami the following year, I immediately thought of Melissa Summerford. I accepted that she didn't have the widest knowledge of Kami and that I would have to spend time training her on the nuances of the app. However, I wouldn't have to spend any time teaching Melissa how to be dynamic, engaging, and authentic – all necessary traits to gain teacher buy-in to learn Kami. As predicted, she soared in her interviews and was hired exactly a year after we first met. When she logged on to our first Zoom meeting, I was shocked at how sterile she seemed. That's why I questioned her use of the headset. "Just be yourself" was the theme of our first couple of weeks together.

It was in her third week at Kami that I noticed a shift in Melissa. While observing one of her virtual workshops, I noticed the headset was gone; Melissa replaced it with a bright velvet headband covered with beaded pearls. I also noticed her more relaxed instructional style that felt much more like the Melissa I met a year prior. At one point in the session, she meandered into a personal tangent about her love of Taylor Swift. I smiled throughout the entire presentation because Melissa felt relatable and inspiring. I even caught myself abandoning my observation notes so that I could participate in her discussions and activities. When she and I had a chance to debrief, I asked her, "What happened to the headset?" She replied, "I just... stopped wearing it. As I was getting ready for the training, I was so focused on researching my audience and making sure our workshop would be engaging that I didn't even think about the headset." This was the beginning of Melissa Summerford's most authentic chapter in education leadership.

In the year since shedding her headset, Melissa Summerford has delivered her first keynote speech, and she's been recruited to coach at Google for Education Champions Symposium. She's also been nominated for ISTE's (International Society for Technology in Education) Top 20 to Watch Award. Well known for her candid social media posts about her struggles with imposter syndrome and insecurities as a teacher leader, Melissa Summerford is becoming the epitome of elevation through authenticity.

The story of Melissa Summerford is a powerful reminder that sometimes we need to break free from traditional norms and expectations in order to unlock our true potential. In Melissa's case, it was the simple act of shedding her headset during virtual presentations that allowed her to become a more authentic, engaging, and inspiring teacher leader. By letting go of the belief that the headset was the most professional way to host online meetings, Melissa was able to embrace her own unique style and personality, which ultimately led to greater success and recognition in her field.

Of course, this doesn't mean that we should all throw away our headsets or abandon other traditional practices without good reason. Rather, it's a reminder that we should always be willing to question our assumptions and experiment with new approaches in order to find what works best for us and the people we serve. Whether we're teachers, business professionals, or anyone else seeking to make a positive impact in the world, it's important to remember that authenticity and connection are often more powerful than conformity and perfection. By being ourselves and letting our true selves shine through, we can inspire others and achieve great things.

As we reach the culmination of our journey, it's essential to make a final reflection on the insights and actionable strategies we've explored. This guide has been more than a manual; it's been a companion in your quest to revolutionize teacher training. The narrative we've woven from the preface to the intricate details of knowing your audience, designing impactful presentations, mastering public speaking, navigating the virtual teaching landscape, and pursuing relentless professional growth, all aim to empower you, the Teacher Trainer.

As you move forward, armed with the knowledge and strategies from this guide, remember that the journey of improvement is perpetual. The landscape of education and professional development is ever-evolving, and so should our approaches to teacher training. Continue to experiment, reflect, and adapt, always with the aim of fostering environments where learning thrives.

In conclusion, this book is a call to action. It challenges you to look beyond the content and focus on the delivery, the engagement, and the transformative power you hold. As you turn the final page of this guide, consider it not the end but a new beginning in your journey to elevate teacher training. Your journey to delivering elevated PD is just beginning; the future is ripe with possibilities. Here's to creating learning experiences that resonate, inspire, and endure.

Appendix

Transferrable Teacher Tips

TABLE A.1 All 15 Transferable Teacher Tips from throughout the book

Transferable Teacher Tip #1: Plan to Greet

Similar to standing in the hallway of your classroom and greeting students as they enter, position yourself so that you're able to greet teachers with a warm welcome. Reserve time and space in your plans to greet.

Transferable Teacher Tip #2: Be the First to Say "Hello!"

Teachers take the lead when greeting students and initiating the lesson, so do the same with adults. Remember that your greeting is both a disarming tool and a way to check the pulse of your learners, so don't wait to be smiled at; smile first.

Transferable Teacher Tip #3: Be a De-escalator

Classroom teachers experience communication conflicts regularly, especially when it comes to student misbehavior. Remember that the best way to calm the conversation is to de-escalate. Maintain a calm communication style when presenting even when conversations become tense.

Transferable Teacher Tip #4: Don't Reinvent the Wheel

Classroom teachers are expert hunters and gatherers when it comes to sourcing readymade instructional materials. The same applies to teacher leaders. The next time you're charged with delivering an original training session, search the internet first. There's a high likelihood that you'll at least find a starting point of inspiration.

Transferable Teacher Tip #5: Let the Conversation Meander…Just a Little

It happens all the time in the classroom – an excited student's discussion veers off into a tangent. This happens with adult learners too. Instead of immediately stifling the excitement, allow the moment of joy to fill the room before getting the conversation back on track.

Transferable Teacher Tip #6: If Possible, Study Your Roster

Each year, classroom teachers receive rosters of students and some form of their previous education information. The same applies to the rosters of teachers who sign up for your training sessions. If you can capture audience information before the training, research their subject areas, grade levels, extra-curricular involvement, and accolades. These are all potential relevancy drivers for your scheduled training.

(Continued)

TABLE A.1 (Continued)

Transferable Teacher Tip #7: Teacher Mode: Activate!

You're not shy when it comes to leading a group of young people, so try to use that same confidence when speaking in front of adults. The core of your confidence in public speaking is the same as the one that helped you excel in teaching students in the classroom.

Transferable Teacher Tip #8: Lost? Find Your Anchor

In the classroom, anchor charts are visual resources that help keep the learning on track. Use this same strategy when you're speaking to teachers. If you fear getting lost in your training, create an easy-to-access visual to remind you of your main points.

Transferable Teacher Tip #9: QTIP (Quit Taking It Personally)

From the way we dress to the way we pronounce certain words, our students find ways to disrupt or even poke fun at us, but we never take it personally. "They're kids," we often say to ourselves. Apply this same level of grace when your trainings get disrupted. Don't take it personal. Stay confident, and deliver that lesson!

Transferable Teacher Tip #10: Get to the Class Early

It's always wise to arrive in your classroom with ample time to prepare the room for learners, and the same applies to your virtual classroom. Allow ample time before your sessions to make sure all of the virtual setup components are in place and functioning properly.

Transferable Teacher Tip #11: Dress for Success

Just because you'll be presenting on camera, that doesn't mean that your attire won't impact training outcomes. Similar to the way your in-person teaching wardrobe is professional with components of personality, so should the outfits you wear on camera. In most cases, your upper body will be the only part of you visible on camera, so take extra care choosing what you wear from the waist up.

Transferable Teacher Tip #12: Use Technology to Visualize Real-Time Responses

In the classroom, teachers ask students ad hoc questions in every lesson. Keep this effective strategy to check for understanding in your virtual workshops by using the web meeting chat or polling add-on to quickly gather audience feedback.

Transferable Teacher Tip #13: Reflect During Your Commute

On your commute, your mind is already teeming with thoughts of work, so make this time intentional. Spend a few minutes of this time affirming yourself by thinking of the positive practices you've exhibited recently.

(Continued)

TABLE A.1 (Continued)

Transferable Teacher Tip #14: Share Your Work Online

You already use social media to consume the information you're looking for, so spend some of that online time looking for growth through peer feedback. Share work and ideas online and request feedback from your peers. If you're brave enough to post a selfie, you're brave enough to share your expertise.

Transferable Teacher Tip #15: Organize Your Learnings

Teachers store and organize instructional materials so that they can easily be sourced and implemented based on the needs of the students. Think of your professional growth materials the same way. Take a moment to make sure you can easily locate, skim, and scan your personal library of teachable trainer moments.

Putting it into Action Choice Mega Choice Board

TABLE A.2 Putting it All Together activities consolidated into a single choice board

Reflect	Explore	Experiment
Create a superhero persona for yourself based on your ideal communicator traits. How can you bring out your inner communication superhero in your interactions with colleagues? What does it take for you to go from Clark Kent to Superman?	Use an AI chatbot like ChatGPT to generate creative ways to improve your andragogy. In your query, use modifiers like "creative" and "out of the box" to generate more innovative ideas.	Create three new ways to get your audience's attention without speaking like a scolding parent or a complaining child ego. Remember that communication can be verbal or nonverbal.
Perform a rigidity check on your most recent training. As you presented, how frequently did you adjust your pace or depth of content delivery? How often did the audience lead instruction? What adjustments can you make in the future to plan for a less linear delivery of information?	Use an AI chatbot to search for more easy-to-visualize audience prompts that you can use during trainings. Which prompts tend to yield the most informative insights while being the least disruptive to the flow of your workshop?	Choose a nonverbal audience cue to look for in your next training. Try responding to the cue in more than one way. Which response was the most effective? Why do you think so?

(Continued)

TABLE A.2 (Continued)

Reflect	Explore	Experiment
Become a fear fighter by first listing your top three public speaking fears. Next, list the top three things teachers value about your training. The next time one of your fears creeps in, fight them by reminding yourself of your top three points of value.	Search YouTube for other Teacher Trainers confidently discussing similar topics as you. How can you tell the person is confident? Which strategies from Chapter 3 do you think the presenter has used to become a confident speaker?	Instead of rehearsing your presentations in first person, try practicing them as narratives told in the third person point of view. As the narrator of your presentation, diagram your story's plot by clearly defining the conflict, rising action, climax, falling action, and conclusion. What new thoughts surface when you think of your presentation in plot sequence format?
The next time you get an opportunity to watch someone else present virtually, write down all of the visual elements you love. What about these visual elements that made you love them?	Virtual presentation tools are constantly evolving. To become more familiar with the software you use for virtual presentations, search YouTube for tutorials, tips, and tricks.	Include personal artifacts or wear your favorite outfit in your next virtual training. Naturally embed them as talking points to share more about who you are as a person. Document how this made you feel and how the audience reacted.
Take a journey to your future self, ten years from now. What creative teaching practices have become your trademark? What insights or advice does your future self offer regarding cultivating creative thinking skills?	Use Table 5.2 to perform a refined social media search for conversations about soft skills beyond creative and analytical thinking. How many new soft skills upskilling sources can you identify?	Volunteer to serve on the planning committee of the next education conference or meeting you plan to attend. Use this as an opportunity to fellowship with peers and unearth new potential mentors.

For Product Safety Concerns and Information please contact our
EU representative GPSR@taylorandfrancis.com Taylor & Francis
Verlag GmbH, Kaufingerstraße 24, 80331 München, Germany